Natchez

Other books by Hugh Howard

The Williamsburg House
Thomas Jefferson Architect (with Roger Straus III)
House-Dreams
Wright for Wright (with Roger Straus III)
The Preservationist's Progress
How Old Is This House?

Other books by Roger Straus III

Thomas Jefferson, Architect (with Hugh Howard)
Wright for Wright (with Hugh Howard)
Modernism Reborn: Mid-Century American Houses
(with Michael Webb)
U. S. 1: America's Original Main Street
(with Andrew H. Malcolm)
Mississippi Currents (with Andrew H. Malcolm)

Seen from the east through its luxuriant gardens, Peter Little's Rosalie.

Natchez

THE HOUSES AND HISTORY OF THE JEWEL OF THE MISSISSIPPI

Text by Hugh Howard   *Photography by Roger Straus III*

RIZZOLI
NEW YORK

For
Elizabeth Anne Howard
H. H.

For

The Citizens of Natchez

with gratitude, admiration and some envy.
R. S.

First published in the United States of America in 2003 by
Rizzoli International Publications, Inc.
300 Park Avenue South
New York, NY 10010
www.rizzoliusa.com

2008/ 10 9 8 7 6 5 4 3

Designed by Doris Straus

Printed in China

ISBN-13: 978-0-8478-2572-1

Library of Congress Catalog Control Number: 2003110708

Author's Note

Natchez is a town enraptured by its own history. Tourists come to absorb a sense of a bygone past, and the denizens of Natchez strive to offer them the experience they seek. For Natchezians and their guests, this is a place where few focus on the future.

Natchez – the name is pronounced *NATCH-iz* as in *matches* – has a genteel feel. Life in this small city is understood to be a function of the past, largely because it was a grand and elegant past. Beginning about 1800, a great wave of wealth transformed a frontier settlement into the opulent town that survives today, and the character of the place is still defined by the half-dozen decades that preceded the Civil War.

Essential to Natchez's charm is the palpable presence of history. You can't escape it, any more than you can avoid the heat and humidity. Indeed, the languid pace of the place is part of its appeal, with its hot, humid, semitropical climate of sixty inches of rain per year and temperatures in the nineties for months on end. The climate certainly slows you down, but perhaps that only helps one better appreciate the picture-book collection of grand mansions that is Natchez's greatest asset. The houses and the streetscapes lure tens of thousands of visitors each year; they come to admire not only the architecture but the furnishings and decorations. Countless objects remain in the homes for which they were purchased back in the early-to-mid-nineteenth century, and the same constancy is reflected in the inhabitants. Many have family trees firmly rooted in Natchez soil, and a few of them still live in the homes their ancestors built before the Civil War.

The aim of this book is to capture some sense of Natchez in words and pictures. That task is not a simple one, given the rich and complex history of this riverfront town. After all, Natchez is both the oldest continuous settlement on the Mississippi River and the place where Jerry Lee Lewis, who grew up across the river, first played for money at the Hilltop Club in 1949. It is a town of towering magnolia trees and live oaks with Spanish moss swaying off the branches like featherdusters. It was a big-time boomtown that went bust; but somehow the place has survived against the odds, having been buffeted by war, economic downturns, tornadoes, and radical social change. It's a great oral history town in a region where such places abound; but the stories, inevitably, keep coming full circle to bring us back to the houses.

Natchez is nothing if not a house-proud town. On one of my early visits I was given a driving tour full of stops and starts. My guide would come to a halt in the middle of the street. He'd point at a grand house, then commence to gesticulate and talk at length about the building, its history, perhaps its inhabitants. Even as I craned my neck to see what he was pointing at, I noticed that cars would come up behind us, pause a moment, then simply drive around us. No one ever honked, not one person. Obviously, the obstacle before them was familiar (and not altogether unwelcome). It was just another gawker, lookin' at and admirin' the houses of Natchez.

In most towns, people identify houses by association with past or present occupants. In Natchez, too, the houses have names, but few are of families. Most are evocative names like *Magnolia Hall, Auburn, Longwood, Edgewood,* and *Cottage Gardens.* Others are vaguely allusive or obscure, like *Gloucester, Monteigne, Rosalie,* or *Hope Farm.* But do not be confused — names *are* important. When I asked one Natchezian about a particular house that had caught my eye driving around town, he sniffed, "It doesn't even have a name." As if that meant the place was unworthy of attention.

Each of our visits to Natchez left our memories awash not only with the names of houses, but with people, images, and objects. The task left us was to impose our own framework on the place. That we have tried to do but, admittedly, our view is not the only one. There are other worthy houses that might have been included, but the choices we made reflect what Roger Straus and I, as photographer and writer, respectively, understand to be the character of the place.

Like the lines on an aging face, the streetscapes of Natchez can be read to reveal much about its history. Some reflect the developmental pressures produced by the automobile. The strip development on the outskirts meant that downtown theaters, shops, and stores closed, reducing a once-vital business district — like countless others across the country — to an unnatural quietude. There are signs of growth on the suburban streets, too, where bungalows, ranch houses, and split-levels have appeared not so many blocks from the business district downtown. But invariably the line of post-World War II houses is broken by an immense mansion, an edifice of a scale and grandeur that turns the clock back a century and a half in time.

The mansion houses are what make Natchez the memorable place that it is; those houses that represent its citizens' allegiance to the past. For us, these sites, the tour guides, and the city itself collectively bridge the deep and distant gap that separates our time from antebellum Natchez.

–Hugh Howard

Photographer's Note

Natchez casts a spell. The traveller feels transported to a glorious nineteenth-century city. As a photographer, I wondered, if in order to capture the spirit of this meticulously preserved place, I should be working with materials from the period, something along the lines of glass-plate negatives.

This book's printer will be relieved to know that I came to my senses, and instead of glass-plate negatives, I shot Fujichrome Provia 100F and 400F. I loaded the film into two contemporary cameras – a Linhof Technorama 617 S with a Schneider Super-Angulon 5.6/90 lens, and a Silvestri T-30 with a Schneider Super-Angulon XL 5.6/47 lens.

Even though I forsook nineteenth-century equipment, I hope the unique character of Natchez has been preserved.

-Roger Straus

Above:
Natchez City Cemetery

Preceding pages:
Despite its commanding river view, Natchez is isolated. Until 1940 no bridge crossed the Mississippi River at Natchez, so ferries were the means of delivering people and goods back and forth across the river.

Contents

In the nineteenth century — the black-and-white photograph (above) dates from 1861 — Natchez Under-the-Hill was a town unto itself at
the base of the bluff. Today (below) the Mississippi has eroded it to a narrow strip of land and a single row of structures at the river's edge.
Collection of Thomas H. Gandy and Joan W. Gandy.

Introduction

The history of a place can be usually condensed into a sequence of governmental actions. A summary view, then, of political events in the early days of Natchez goes this way.

A Native American tribe, the Natchez Indians, had inhabited the area for centuries when the Spanish conquistador Hernando de Soto came searching for El Dorado. He didn't find it, and instead died from an infected wound a few miles north of the present city in 1542. In 1682 another European visitor arrived, the French explorer La Salle (René Robert Cavelier, Sieur de La Salle). He befriended the Natchez Indians before proceeding on to what would become New Orleans.

The first European settlement in the area wasn't established until 1714, when a band of Frenchmen set up a trading post at the river's edge. Two years later a military force constructed Fort Rosalie on the two-hundred-foot-tall-bluff overlooking the river. Within a decade some 6,000 acres were in cultivation in the Natchez district, but the Natchez Indians, their ranks already decimated by infectious diseases carried by the earlier European arrivals, resisted further displacement from their lands. They made their last stand in 1729, attacking the French community and killing perhaps a third of its seven hundred inhabitants. The military retaliation annihilated the tribe, effectively bringing an end to the Natchez Indian culture.

A few soldiers and fur traders came and went in the years that followed, but thirty years would pass before there was a second European habitation at what would eventually become the city of Natchez. This time the Europeans wore British uniforms, as the Treaty of Paris in 1763 had ceded control of the territory to George III. Fort Panmure was constructed on the site of Fort Rosalie, and numerous land grants gave British veterans of the French and Indian War substantial holdings in the vicinity. Then in 1779 British troops surrendered Fort Panmure to a Spanish force, and Spain governed the region for most of the next twenty years.

The population grew during and after the American Revolution. Loyalists to Britain escaped there from the colonies, many of them arriving by foot on the now-legendary Natchez Trace, a 450-mile-long trail from Nashville that was the main overland means of reaching Natchez. The population was diverse, with inhabitants who could claim French, Spanish, British, and American origins. By the early 1780s Natchez was a rural settlement with a population of about five

hundred, roughly double the number of its inhabitants in 1776. Most resided on their farms, but a fraction of them lived in the small settlement of log houses that had sprouted below the bluff, just above the level of the Mississippi. The river bank there became a rough-and-tumble community known as Natchez Under-the-Hill.

The Spanish governor hired John Girault to lay out the town grid on top of the hill about 1791. Finally, in 1798 the United States assumed formal control and by an act of Congress the area became the Mississippi Territory. In 1803 Natchez was incorporated as a town and Mississippi became a state in 1817.

The politics tell only part of the story. A more elemental confluence of events may better explain the dynamic changes that shaped the isolated region roughly a hundred miles north of the Gulf of Mexico. Ranking higher than mere politics in determining the subsequent development of Natchez are geographical factors (including fertile soils, abundant rainfall, and the presence of the great river), as well as technological change.

The Natchez Indians had practiced subsistence agriculture, planting the "three sisters" (corn, beans, and squash), but the first Europeans almost immediately cultivated crops that could be turned into profit. The French settlers exported wheat and tobacco, as well as lumber products. The British traded cattle and horses, but at the instigation of the Spanish the

The view looking north from the Natchez bluff of the broad, winding Mississippi River.

local farmers began to produce indigo, the herb from which blue dye is made. While some cotton was grown, more profitable crops dominated until a Yankee tinkerer, working as a tutor at Mulberry Grove, a plantation in Georgia, made possible a radical transformation of the agricultural economy in the South.

Eli Whitney was clever with machinery, and in 1793 he tried his hand at improving the cotton gin. The existing device was of little use in separating the vegetable fibers from the seeds in the capsule (or "boll"), but in a mere ten days Whitney is said to have devised the first version of his cotton gin. He was granted a patent for his design and his efficient and easy-to-replicate machine was soon appearing all over the map.

In 1794 Natchez produced fewer than forty thousand pounds of cotton. The following year, however, the first cotton gin arrived in the region, making large-scale processing of cotton possible. Within five years annual cotton exports were up to three *million* pounds of cotton, departing the docks at Natchez Under-the-Hill on flatboats. The mode of transport would change after 1811 when the *New Orleans* initiated steamboat service to its namesake city. Natchez quickly became the preeminent port in the Mississippi Territory. The steamers delivered cotton fibers, already seeded and baled, to New Orleans and beyond. The same ships also brought to Natchez supplies, immigrants — and slaves.

Slavery was a fact of life in antebellum Natchez. The unadorned truth is that the town's wealth and prosperity was a direct consequence of a labor force that consisted almost entirely of enslaved African Americans brought from Virginia and the Carolinas or imported directly from West Africa. The cotton economy was based upon growing, harvesting, ginning, and baling cotton, but even with the advent of the gin, producing cotton was a labor-intensive business. Slaves, lots of them, did the bulk of the work, which made them an economic reality. To the planters, they seemed an economic necessity.

To the twenty-first-century conscience the very thought of slavery is intolerable, yet to apply our ethos is to take the easy way out. We may regard the planters of Natchez as violators of what now seems a natural law, namely, the prohibition of involuntary servitude on the basis of race. But turning away in disgust means denying the very real paradigm of the time. In that era, slavery had the official sanction of not only the state of Mississippi but the United States of America.

Slavery had actually shown signs of waning in the early decades of the nineteenth century in much of the country, having been abandoned in the Northern states. But this gradual change hadn't come about because of the high rhetoric of the abolitionists; that would come later. Rather, slavery was becoming uneconomical, even in other parts of the South; but that was before the cotton boom, when enslaved labor emerged as essential. Like it or not, slavery is a part of the economic history of the South and, by extension, of the North. Much of the cotton was taken there to be processed; many of the planters were Yankees who adopted with alacrity the practice of slavery on their way to wealth; there were free black men, too, who owned slaves. This history is vexing and complex but whatever our feelings about slavery may be today, it was an undeniable reality then.

For the planters in and around Natchez, it was but one of the constants in a formula that produced a result they very much desired. The cultivation of cotton offered, plain and simple, a means of getting very, very rich.

The rapid accumulation of wealth produced an infrastructure. A hospital was built in 1805 and a market house the following year. In 1811 Jefferson College opened in nearby Washington, and in 1818 a women's college, the Elizabeth Female Academy, welcomed its first students. A fire company was organized in 1814. A public school, the Natchez Institute, was established much later, in 1845. The 1820s saw the construction of impressive Episcopal and Presbyterian churches, along with a Masonic Hall. Hotels, banks, and other churches prospered. In 1829 a theater was built. P.T. Barnum came to town, bringing Tom Thumb and Jenny Lind, known as "the Swedish nightingale." Many newspapers came and went, though two competing papers, the *Courier* and the *Free Trader*, endured.

Despite Natchez's rapid development, the place inevitably retained something of its frontier-town character. It remained a rough-and-ready river town with its dockside district, Natchez Under-the-Hill, famed for its violence. The more sophisticated settlement on the hill was certainly a calmer and more cosmopolitan place, but the get-rich-quick nature of Natchez inevitably attracted risk-takers.

Many came from the North, from Pennsylvania, Massachusetts, New York, and Ohio, others from Virginia and Maryland. While more than a few were well educated, most were also men on the make. The untamed nature of the west attracted adventurers of all sorts, and duels, fights, and other violent behaviors associated with emerging western towns were commonplace in the early decades of the nineteenth century, in Natchez as elsewhere. But the higher economic stakes in Natchez attracted more sophisticated adventurers, too, and the stories are legion of young men who disembarked at Natchez to look around – only to stay permanently to try to make their fortune in this boomtown. Certainly some of them frequented gambling tables and horse races; in fact, Natchez became home to a number of men who maintained and raced their own thoroughbred horses. But the real high-stakes game in town was cotton.

A simple means of assessing worldly success in antebellum Natchez was a planter's cotton output. One benchmark for early success was 100 bales a year, the likely yield of about 75 plantation acres. The price of cotton rose and fell, sometimes dramatically, ranging from under 10 cents a pound to several times that. Yet that seemed to add excitement to the

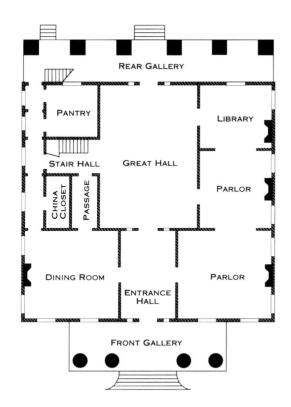

The floor plan of the 1823 house called Rosalie (see page 77) features a characteristic Natchezian touch. There are double parlors, front-to-back, on one side, and there's the familiar central passage — center hall houses were commonplace in the young United States of America by the early nineteenth century. However, in other parts of the country — say, Virginia or New England — a five-bay house like this one would typically have had a grand stairway in the hall. But not at Rosalie. In a variation that became characteristic of many of Natchez's monumental houses (including Melrose and Stanton Hall; see pages 131 and 167), Rosalie's builder turned the stairs ninety degrees and backed them out of the hall into a space between the library and the dining room.

game. In an average year, the proceeds from the sale of 100 bales (a bale consisted of approximately 400 pounds of ginned cotton) might amount to several thousands of dollars in net income; in a year when prices were higher, that profit might be doubled or trebled. The land still had to be paid for, of course, as did the slaves who planted and harvested the cotton (a healthy slave could be counted upon to produce 7 or 8 bales a year), but for people of means and connections, there was easy credit available to purchase the land and "chattel." Repayment would come later, when the cotton was harvested and sold, and often over a period of years. If the slaves were paid for in, say, three years and the land over a longer term, remaining annual profits could then be reinvested to buy more land and more slaves. Over a still longer period, the land, slaves, and anticipated profits could be leveraged repeatedly. Thus a 100-bale planter could aspire to become a 1,000-bale planter. And that meant great wealth, worldly wealth by any standard.

Initially the cotton was grown in and around Natchez. As the one-crop economy began to deplete local soils of nutrients in the 1820s, the holdings of the Natchez planters extended across the river to Concordia Parish, Louisiana, and upstream onto the broad flat acres of the Mississippi delta. Adventurous planters invested still further afield, establishing plantations in Arkansas and even east Texas.

Growing cotton wasn't left solely to the second and third generation of planters with established landholdings; new arrivals in Natchez — lawyers, bankers, doctors, and merchants — invested their earnings in land and grew cotton, too. These men saw that modest profits earned in their original pursuits could be multiplied exponentially. For the most successful the financial returns were almost unbelievable. By the 1850s, the richest of them owned thousands of acres and hundreds of slaves. By the beginning of the Civil War, Natchez had more millionaires per capita than any other city in the country.

Just as there was a formula for getting rich, there became an accepted means for displaying one's accumulated wealth. With Natchez as the cultural and social center of their lives, the planters built themselves grand estates on the perimeter of the town or mansions on the downtown grid. Taken together, the *villa suburbana* and the in-town *palazzi* constitute perhaps the single most impressive concentration of high-style architecture from the antebellum era to be seen anywhere.

The architecture of Natchez evolved along with the economics of cotton. Simple frontier dwellings — a single room, then two separated by a hall — were succeeded by larger houses in a vernacular style adapted to the subtropical climate (see Chapter 1, *The Planter's House*, page 21). With the rapid growth in cotton profits, larger mansions began to appear. Simple porches were replaced by porticoes supported by classical columns. Builders from England, Ireland, and all over the northern United States came to Natchez to find work. They brought with them architectural trends popular in the fashionable cities on the East Coast. The Federal style became popular (see Chapter 2, *Academic Architecture Arrives*, page 55); it was superseded by the Grecian in the late 1830s (Chapter 3, *The Grecian Mode*, page 89). By the 1850s the Italianate and other Victorian styles were beginning to appear (Chapter 4, *A More Modern Miscellany*, page 153). The houses got larger and more impressive; older houses were updated; and the contents grew more elaborate as the owners returned from their travels to New Orleans, New York, and Europe bearing goods. Natchez had everything that money could buy.

The finest houses of Natchez are tangible symbols of the extraordinary financial success, as well as the excesses, of the antebellum era. The images in the pages that follow portray more than two dozen major houses, and the stories of each are recounted. Taken together, they constitute a key part of the larger narrative of Natchez during the boom before the Civil War.

The boom was followed by a harrowing bust, a consequence of the Civil War, the emancipation of the slaves, crop failures, and a reliance upon King Cotton. While Natchez might well have gone into a precipitous decline, a mixture of pride, stubbornness, and residual wealth kept the place alive. Families in Natchez valiantly soldiered on, attempting to maintain their properties. It was a bitter time, as the large suburban holdings were gradually subdivided, dependencies fell into disuse, and the grand homes deteriorated. Some properties were sold and resold, a few burned, others were abandoned or demolished. Remarkably, however, a surprising number of the fifty-odd major houses survived intact.

By the turn of the twentieth century, a few outsiders began to arrive in Natchez, lured in part by the fine antebellum mansions. A handful of other arrivals in the twenties were harbingers of an early preservation movement that would eventually prove to be the town's salvation. Not that the move to preserve the town came from without — in fact, it was the ladies of Natchez who made preservation a key business in their town.

The economics of Natchez had changed radically, but the appearance of its homes and streetscapes had not. Recognizing this, the Natchez Garden Club sponsored its first annual Garden Pilgrimage Week in 1932. There was one precedent, the Historic Garden Week that had been established in 1929 by the Garden Club of Virginia. But the prime

The ladies of the club — the Natchez Garden Club, to be exact — posed during a Pilgrimage meeting in 1932. That's Katherine Grafton Miller, fifth from the left. Collection of Thomas H. Gandy and Joan W. Gandy.

mover behind the Natchez Pilgrimage, Katherine Grafton Miller, took her pitch on the road. She worked tirelessly to market the Pilgrimage, promoting the event under the rubric "Natchez, Where the Old South Still Lives."

The pilgrims who came to visit the twenty-six houses on the tour got an eyeful. Many of the houses were filled with museum-quality objects and, just as important, they were illuminated by stories. The old South did indeed live on, at least in the memories of many of the women who guided the tours in antebellum garb. This tradition of dressing up in fine gowns — it survives today — probably means Natchez has more women adept at maneuvering in hoopskirts than any place on earth.

One of the more bizarre attempts to market Natchez's past is the incongruously named "Isle of Capri." It's a gaming boat (a barge, really, as it's motorless) moored in the Mississippi at the base of the Natchez bluff.

The now-familiar house tour has become a staple of civic groups across the country, but in Natchez the Pilgrimage became almost a civic duty. Over the years a second garden club was formed, the Pilgrimage Garden Club, and then a third, the Auburn Garden Club. Initially the tour was of the domiciles of the house-proud ladies running the tour, the well-maintained private homes of Natchez. Then in 1935 the Natchez Garden Club took title to a home of its own, the dilapidated 1798 Connelly's Tavern (subsequently renamed the House on Ellicott's Hill). It would be the first public restoration of a house in Natchez. The club stabilized and restored the House on Ellicott's Hill as a museum, then constructed a clubhouse and swimming pool in order to use it as their headquarters and the focus of their social activities.

In 1938 the Pilgrimage Garden Club acquired Stanton Hall, an immense Greek Revival mansion, and it became a museum and that club's home base. That same year the Mississippi State Society of the Daughters of the American Revolution purchased Rosalie, a fine Federal mansion, complete with its 1850s furnishings, in order to open it as a museum. Other acquisitions followed, so that today at least eight fine homes are held in trust for public viewing.

The garden clubs were joined by a different kind of organization in 1974. The Historic Natchez Foundation is a nonprofit preservation organization that has also worked to facilitate the survival of endangered properties (as its director likes to say, "the Historic Natchez Foundation is a sort of humane society for unwanted buildings"). But the foundation has developed a substantial body of research that distinguishes the myth from the reality — and Natchez has its share of myths, having been forced to live off its memories for so long. Rather than relying on arbitrary change and circumstances to preserve the landmarks of Natchez, the foundation has managed to purchase and resell a number of endangered properties, attaching to them preservation easements. It helped establish a historic district around the old Spanish grid in 1979 and got many buildings entered on the National Register of Historic Places.

Still another presence in the movement to preserve Natchez arrived in 1988 when an act of Congress established the Natchez National Historical Park. The Park Service then acquired several properties in Natchez, ranging from the property known as Melrose, with its important Greek Revival mansion and landscape, to the William Johnson House, a brick townhouse built for a free black businessman in 1841.

Through a combination of factors — among them the growth of tourism, the national preservation movement, and the emergence of material culture as an academic discipline — there is now a more rigorous approach to restoration efforts in Natchez. Yet much credit must go to the gracious ladies in costume during Pilgrimage, then and now. If it hadn't been for the decades of energy brought by the members of the garden clubs and the attention that the Pilgrimage brought to the antebellum mansions, the genteel air of another era might well have been lost. Natchez might have devolved into a very different place indeed, rather than becoming what it is, a unique example of living history.

In the formal front parlor at The Briars hangs a portrait of Jefferson Davis, later President of the Confederate States. Varina Howell, who grew up here, and Davis were married in this room in 1845.

CHAPTER I

The Planter's House

———— ⌘ ————

HOPE FARM

AIRLIE

TEXADA

THE HOUSE ON ELLICOTT'S HILL

THE BRIARS

"The houses are chiefly framed buildings; but though this country has been settled so long, there is all that inattention to neatness, cleanliness, and the comfort attending thereon, that there is in a country just cleared."
Francis Baily, *Journal of a Tour in Unsettled Parts of North America*, 1797

The earliest buildings in Natchez are long gone. The first shops and dwellings built both at Natchez Under-the-Hill and on the first established farms were one-room structures called single-pen houses. They consisted of little more than four walls notched together at the corners to form one room roughly twenty feet square. Typically these simple frontier dwellings had gable roofs, a chimney on one end, and doors at the front and back. As time and material allowed, the so-called dog-trot configuration developed. These houses consisted of two pens separated by an open passageway but covered by a single roof.

As the planters became more prosperous, porches (traditionally called "galleries" in Natchez) were added to capture the summer breezes. These galleries often lined the backs as well as the fronts of the planters' homes. These early houses telegraph their evolution: The original roof had one pitch, the add-on gallery roof a second, flatter slope. Later houses, often built in one campaign, typically had a single roofline extending from the peak to the eave of the gallery in one unbroken slope. Two houses featured in this chapter, Airlie and The Briars, are examples of these two types (see pages 31 and 47, respectively).

The earliest houses were plain in the extreme, as the goal was little more than shelter and safety. Yet in the developmental way of so much native architecture, the essence of the early structures can be seen in later, fancier Natchez architecture. In particular, the central open passage proved to be a precedent. The passage, which was open on the ends but sheltered from the sun, became a highly practical space, one in which much of the life of the house was lived. It had multiple uses — eating, working, relaxing, and even sleeping were done there to take advantage of cooling breezes. The open passageway thus

The Grecian style dining room at the Anglo-Spanish Hope Farm

anticipated the much grander enclosed central hall of the mansions that followed, an adaptive use seen earlier in Virginia as well, where the airy central passage had become a place for summer living in the eighteenth century, and was even referred to in documents of the time as the "summer hall." As finances allowed or logistics required, second stories were also added.

The architecture of Natchez evolved over the decades, but even as styles changed building practices had a number of constants. Most of the materials were local, pest-resistant cypress milled from nearby forests and bricks made of local clay. The overall schema, though subject to significant variations, reflected the subtropical climate. Most houses — whether Federal, Grecian, or Italianate — had tall ceilings, large rooms, the ubiquitous central hall, and gallery porches or porticoes that offered protection from the sun and torrential rains. Detached kitchens were another practical consideration, given the heat in the summer, the risk of fire, and the ample supply of servants.

A bedchamber at the House on Ellicott's Hill with its display of children's furniture.

The oldest surviving houses in Natchez include the five featured in this chapter. Three of those represent the era of Spanish governance (Hope Farm, Airlie, and Texada; see pages 25, 31, and 35, respectively); another, the House on Ellicott's Hill, is a unique amalgam of Caribbean and lower Mississippi valley influences (page 41); the fifth, The Briars, suggests much about how the Natchez style would evolve in the early years of the nineteenth century (page 47). These are not the sort of high-style houses that adorn the covers of style books. They're more ordinary houses — scholars term them "vernacular" architecture — that were built more simply by builders who constructed other, similar houses to suit local needs and limitations. If part of the pleasure in examining historic houses comes from identifying their parentage, then these houses are not only a stepping-off point for a tour of Natchez's finest homes but also offer a glimpse back at the origins of Natchez itself.

Hope Farm

CONSTRUCTED CIRCA 1789
REMODELED CIRCA 1840 AND AFTER 1930

*H*ouses change with the times, and Hope Farm has seen its share of changes. Built in the eighteenth century, it began as an Anglo-Spanish frontier house. Twice in later years it was reinvented and, along the way, it also gained its name. Yet the phases in its evolution have coalesced into a house that is central to both Natchez's early and its more recent history.

Hope Farm is among the oldest structures in Natchez. The precise dates of its construction remain unknown, but certainly Don Carlos de

Hope Farm was once in the countryside. Although two centuries of development brought a wave of other houses, the house still feels isolated sited on its small rise amid its generous fifteen acres.

At Hope Farm, the Williamsburg Room, painted a light Prussian blue, is suggestive of Colonial America with its paneling, furnishings, and, by Natchez standards, small size. The cupboard, made of native cherry and cypress, is thought to have come from a Mississippi plantation.

Grand Pré purchased the property in 1789 and resided there for a dozen years. Though born in France, he was the Spanish commandant at Natchez, leaving his imprint on the town as well as the house, since he helped establish the city grid that survives atop the bluff.

The house that Don Carlos de Grand Pré knew is largely obscured today. Later owners renovated the house, enlarging the simple early structure by adding a deep front gallery across its front and a new wing to the rear. The detailing that was added – moldings, doors, and other woodwork – was executed in the then-current Greek Revival style, probably in the 1840s.

While all of the changes added to the importance of this house, its status probably reached its zenith after Mr. and Mrs. J. Balfour Miller purchased Hope Farm in 1926. It was the redoubtable Katherine Grafton Miller who conceived the

The Planter's House

The two-story rear wing at Hope Farm contains a kitchen and the Williamsburg Room on the ground floor, along with bedrooms above. The sheltering galleries link the two structures.

notion of opening the houses of Natchez as an accompaniment to the state garden club convention in 1931. The experiment was such a success that Mrs. Miller was moved to suggest an even bolder plan: Why not make the house tour an annual event? She worked to promote both Natchez and the Pilgrimage, and herself became a formidable figure in the town.

Her own house has proved an enduring vehicle for interpreting the past. She broadened the "history" at Hope Farm to reflect the trend in the 1930s toward interpreting early houses in a romanticized Colonial manner. She hired a decorator who transformed one space, now known as the Williamsburg Room, giving it paneling, moldings, colors, and the imagined feel of eighteenth-century Tidewater Virginia. What this Colonial Revival approach may have lacked in academic rigor, however, is more than compensated for by the warmth and hospitality of Hope Farm. Under Mrs. Miller's ownership, Hope Farm became the town's first bed-and-breakfast accommodation back in 1932 and remains one today.

The early kitchen at Hope Farm, on display for Pilgrimage, with a range of antique cooking implements.

Opposite top:
The details in the parlor at Hope Farm date from the Greek Revival renovation in the 1840s. The portrait over the piano came much later:
The sitter was Katherine Grafton Miller, founder of the Pilgrimage and lady of the house at Hope Farm for half a century.

Opposite below:
Two beds — a grand "full-tester" (canopy) with a daybed at its foot — in a guest room at Hope Farm.

Airlie

Constructed 1793
remodeled 1832 and after

*S*ome houses in Natchez call attention to themselves. Many of the mansions here are tall and imposing, and their ornamented grandeur attests to the wealth and status of their builders. In contrast, this "Mansion House," despite its historic pedigree, speaks quietly from its gentle rise just north of town.

Airlie is a survivor, a prototypical planter's house dating, in part, from the Spanish era in the early 1790s. The original structure consisted of

The central passage was becoming a fixture in Natchez architecture when the owner of Airlie updated the earlier house. Notice the change in ceiling height, a consequence of the renovation process in the 1830s.

just two rooms over a cellar — at first, there was neither the need nor the means for pretense. Later a more generous room was added across the front, a parlor with a formal entrance. By 1800 the house was substantial enough that a deed transaction that year referred to it as the "Mansion House," though by the later, grander standards of Natchez Airlie remained modest, even after still another section was added, together with an open hallway that linked the older eastern portion of the house to its western wing.

The house that resulted from all these building stages is an elaborate version of the classic dog-trot configuration, with enclosed quarters on either side of a central hall. The breezy openness of the house is enhanced by the sheltering galleries that line the front and the back of the eight-room house, with multiple openings, door and windows, easing access and airflow. The Grecian moldings and millwork in the house date to the 1830s, but the overall character is earlier, thanks to the Spanish influence. At present the walls and ceiling of the earliest portion of the house are open, creating an open kitchen and family room.

The long, low one-story house has become a family home for a couple and their preschool-age son; the lady of the house is a Natchez girl come home, and a member of a younger generation of Natchez women upholding the tradition of Pilgrimage. Airlie is one of Natchez's earliest homes; it is a house that feels of-a-piece, although it has seen a variety of architectural changes, having evolved from a simple planter's home, with significant renovations around 1800, in the 1830s, and later, in the 1850s. Airlie also served as a Union hospital during the Civil War, but today it's a comfortable residence once more, notable in part for its calm setting, just north of the early Spanish grid of downtown Natchez.

The Planter's House

Left:
The difference in roof pitch from the house to the galleries, together with changes in floor and ceiling levels inside the house, help distinguish the various stages in the evolution of Airlie between the 1790s and the 1850s.

Below:
When the owners opened up the walls of the eighteenth-century portion of Airlie, "nogging" was uncovered, a brick infilling between the wooden members of the cypress frame.

Texada

CONSTRUCTED 1798
REMODELED CIRCA 1835, REMODELED 1965 - 1973

*L*ike Airlie, Texada is a survivor of the Spanish era in Natchez, having been built before the turn of the nineteenth century. Yet the two houses could hardly be more different.

Texada is thought to have been Natchez's first brick building. It's an in-town house, neatly aligned with the 1791 plat decreed by the Spanish governor. Texada is an imposing house, its masonry mass standing a full two stories, with a tall attic contained by its steep gable roof.

The original structure was built by an Anglo-American builder, but its name (pronounced *Ta-HAH-dah*) comes from an early owner who

In the dining room at Texada note the exposed beams in the ceiling.

The setting is downtown Natchez, corner of Washington and Wall Streets.

Right:
By the time the restoration of Texada was undertaken, the building had been subdivided into ten small apartments. This image predates the removal of the stucco from the brick walling and the return of the home to a one-family dwelling.
Collection of Thomas H. Gandy and
Joan W. Gandy.

The Planter's House

The rear galleries of Texada (right) face a two-story dependency across the brick-paved courtyard. The owners resided in the dependency for the eight years required to complete the remodeling in the late 1960s and early 1970s.

left his mark. Spaniard Don Manuel Garcia de Texada was a man of means. He had arrived in Natchez about 1781 and prospered as a lawyer and planter, so it's only fitting that the home he built for himself was, according to one contemporary description, a "large elegant and commodious new brick House."

In its early days, Texada wasn't a single-family dwelling. The building was constructed virtually atop the property line, and with its front façade so convenient to the street, Texada's ground floor was well suited for commercial rentals. Among the early tenants were a tailoring business and "Mr. Haughton's Dancing Academy." The house became the American Eagle Tavern after 1806, and in 1817, home to the Mississippi legislature (by then, Texada had been purchased by Judge Edward Turner, the speaker of the House of Representatives). Decades later the house was divided into two side-by-side dwellings, each with its own entrance.

It was a quite dilapidated structure that once again became the home of a single family in the 1960s. The restorers found little original detail left on the first floor, so woodwork salvaged from other Natchez homes, including an elaborate front doorway, was introduced to give it the early nineteenth-century Natchez character it has today. While the front of the house still opens directly

onto the Wall Street sidewalk, there's an enclosed, brick-paved courtyard to the rear. The sense of separation from the street is enhanced by the presence of a gate and a two-story dependency, once the kitchen and servants' quarters. In recent years, the owners of Texada have offered bed-and-breakfast accommodations, a use reminiscent of earlier days when it was a tavern.

The salvaged mantel and chair rail give the room a Federal-era character.

Left:
The frontispiece at Texada is a pedimented doorway that was salvaged from another early Natchez home, Burling Hill, prior to its demolition. Burling Hill has been attributed to Levi Weeks, the architect of Auburn.

The House
on Ellicott's Hill

CONSTRUCTED 1798, 1801
REMODELED CIRCA 1830, RESTORED 1934 AND AFTER

The story of this house is the narrative of Natchez, at least in political and economic terms. Events that unfolded on the site saw the Americans displace the Spanish; the coming and going of numerous players in the city's early history; the habitation by workers in cotton mills; and, finally, the first civic architectural restoration undertaken in Natchez.

The name comes from Andrew Ellicott, the surveyor President George Washington dispatched to lay claim to the Natchez district. Major

The House on Ellicott's Hill was built into the brow of its hill, giving it a two-story elevation looking westward over the Mississippi

A single-story façade faced east, with the main floor of the house opening onto the top of the hill.

Ellicott did as he was ordered, and on February 27, 1797, he raised the flag of the United States on the hilltop where this house stands today. The house itself came later, as did the acquiescence of the Spaniards, who didn't evacuate their installation at Fort Rosalie for another year.

The house that stands on the site of Ellicott's flag waving is not typical of the later elegant dwellings of Natchez: It is, after all, a vestige of frontier days. A merchant named James Moore acquired the property, and the dwelling he built still survives as the nucleus of the House on Ellicott's Hill. At the time of construction in 1798 or after, Moore's house consisted of just two rooms, with a wood-frame living space above a brick basement built into the grade. Some thirty years later rooms were added to each end of the original structure, and a two-story porch was applied to the river front façade. The brick chimneys define the gable ends of the original house, while the newer porches and additions are topped by a lower-pitched hip roof.

The house was subsequently home to the mayor of Natchez; later, to a physician, Dr. Frederick Seip; and, for three decades, to the private Natchez High School for Boys. In 1878 the school closed and the building became a tenement for workers in neighboring cotton mills. By 1934 the building had fallen into disuse and disrepair, and the Natchez Garden Club purchased the property, embarking upon a restoration.

The house is an intriguing anomaly. Despite its galleries, it isn't a true planter's cottage, and architectural historians have debated for years the origins of its design. The inspiration was most likely the Caribbean style found in English West Indian colonies like Antigua, but the uniqueness of this house is also a function of its site.

Today we appreciate the spectacular view of the Mississippi, but in early Natchez the galleries that line the river façade at the House on Ellicott's Hill were important living spaces, used not only for

The Planter's House

The prep room kitchen, like the rest of the house, is furnished with an eclectic array of objects, many of them of Natchez provenance.

socializing but for working, eating, and even sleeping. Every room in the house opens to the exterior; despite the fact that its ceilings don't rise to the heights of later, grander houses, one of the chief virtues of the House on Ellicott's Hill is its airiness, as it welcomes breezes off the river while the wide, hipped roofs over its galleries provide protection from the hot sun and frequent heavy rains of Natchez's subtropical climate.

This was a sturdy and practical house – witness the multiple and diverse uses to which it was put over its long history – but today it has taken on much of the look it had in Natchez's early days.

The furnishings in the House on Ellicott's Hill today are not original to the house, though the objects on display reflect inventories from the residences of former owners James Moore and Frederick Seip. This room, a chamber, features a portrait of the man himself, Major Andrew Ellicott.

The Briars

CONSTRUCTED CIRCA 1818

The plan is familiar enough, with a gallery (or porch) across the front, a row of rooms behind, and a second gallery to the rear. But The Briars is an elaboration on the basic theme of the planter's cottage.

As constructed, The Briars had a central passage or hall, flanked by two symmetrical rooms on each side. Along the axis of five rooms across the front, there are public spaces on either side of the passage (dining room, left, a parlor, right) with outer bedchambers at each end. Across the rear of the building is a second set of spaces, with an open gallery at the center and two small additional rooms or *cabinets*, one at each end, for storage, sleeping, and staircase spaces. Much later, the rear gallery was enclosed to make a grand parlor or sitting room.

The Briars is a planter's cottage with a difference, thanks to the work of its probable builder, Massachusetts-born Levi Weeks.

The spacious front gallery at The Briars. Though the house is wood-framed, the walling visible on the gallery is of stucco.

This house represented a step up the evolutionary ladder in Natchez architecture. The simple planter's cottage with two or three rooms and a pair of porches became a seven-room house. And that's not even counting the generous living spaces incorporated into the tall gable roof, lit by the dormers that line the roof.

The owner of this house was a planter with money to spend, a Marylander named John Perkins. He gained title in October of 1818 to the ninety-nine-acre suburban site with its majestic view of the Mississippi from its tall bluff. But this parcel was far from his only holding, as Perkins amassed some 18,000 cotton-producing acres. His success meant he had the funds to elaborate upon a by-then familiar vernacular floor plan and also to add an array of architectural details.

The Planter's House

The finish is so rich, in fact, that it has been speculated that Perkins hired Levi Weeks, the most sophisticated builder in Natchez at the time, to execute the work. No documentary proof links Weeks to The Briars, but the original millwork, most of which survives, makes the case. Whoever executed the Adam-influenced, American Federal detailing on the mantels, the door and window architraves, and the elliptical fan sash over the doorways had both the skill to shape the wooden elements and the sophisticated knowledge to do it correctly. In the next chapter, we'll get a chance to look at details that are certifiably the work of Levi Weeks at Auburn (see page 67), but the elegant detailing at The Briars serves as a fine introduction to the craftsman's work.

Today The Briars stands on nineteen acres, its original site encroached upon by a modern motel. To reach The Briars, which is open both as a house museum and a bed-and-breakfast inn, the visitor must exit from a divided highway

Above:
The rear gallery at The Briars overlooks a formal garden.

Right:
The dining room at The Briars, its table set with fine glassware, china, and silver.

onto the access road for a Ramada Inn. At the top of the bluff is a standard-issue 1970s motel; beyond, at the back corner of its lot, is a modest sign for The Briars.

   The juxtaposition of the two accommodations is ironic. But then The Briars itself, even when constructed circa 1818, straddled two eras. It had elements of the local vernacular – the house is long and low (the front gallery stretches eighty feet), and its porches are recessed beneath its gable roof. While the shape says "planter's cottage," the detailing is rich and academic, with its classically inspired columns, pilasters, mantels, and architraves. It's a house that summarized much that came before and foreshadowed what was to come.

Left:
The once-open gallery at the rear of the house with its keystoned arcade was enclosed and became a grand parlor.

Below:
The entrance to The Briars had a formality new to Natchez in 1818. The porch supports are no longer just chamfered posts but tapering Doric columns. In this image they frame the delicate elliptical fan sash over the front entrance and support the roof, which in turn is decorated with dormers whose windows have sticking that resembles Gothic tracery.

The house called Rosalie, built 1823.

CHAPTER 2

Academic Architecture Arrives

— ✠ —

GLOUCESTER
AUBURN
LINDEN
ROSALIE
HAWTHORNE

"The houses are extremely irregular and for the most part temporary things. But of late a number of good houses have been built. I last year built an excellent two story brick house . . . [and] in the vicinity of town there is a number of Gentlemen's Seats."
Levi Weeks, designer-builder, in a letter home to Deerfield,
Massachusetts, September 27, 1812

Like Natchez, John James Audubon had something to prove. He was the illegitimate child of a French sea captain and had been jailed as a bankrupt. He had left his wife and sons to embark on a journey because – again, like Natchez – the naturalist and artist had his eyes on the future.

On his first visit in 1820, Audubon's transport was a flatboat meandering down the Mississippi. He carried little more than his artists' materials, a double-barreled gun, and a diary. He was a handsome man, with strong features and a lustrous head of hair; he had a sturdy look to him, and was admired by his contemporaries for his toughness and ability to survive in the woods far from civilization. Ambition was perhaps his biggest burden, as his quest was to paint the birds of America, life-size and from nature, and he was always making drawings. He kept a journal, too, and that routine recording of day-to-day events also contains an accidental record of Natchez as he saw it in the last week of December 1820.

The Mississippi was then the primary means of travel west of the Appalachians, but for Audubon, the river also offered a diverse set of ecosystems as a major bird migration route. Predictably, he noted the birds on his approach to Natchez, recording in his diary, "The carrion Crows first attracted my attention." His river vantage also afforded him a sense of the life below the bluff. "Saw Mills, placed over the ditches . . . [that] serve to furnish the Mills with timbers floated down [to] them from the interior." What he saw was evidence of the Natchez construction boom which produced the high demand for lumber.

Natchez Under-the-Hill, or the "Lower town" as Audubon called it, next drew his attention. His boat came to shore "amongst about 100 More." Natchez was an important stop for travelers on the river, and Audubon noted it consisted largely of "Ware Houses, Grogg, Chops, Decayed Boats." Audubon's observation, terse as it is, nonetheless suggests the nature of the dock district: It was a tightly packed and shabby place, peopled by a transient population of sailors and riffraff.

As Natchez had first come into view, Audubon had been engaged with a drawing, but as he recorded in his diary, "As soon as my drawing was finished, I cleaned and Went to Natchez properly speaking." Once atop the bluff, he described that, too, in his diary. He remarked on the "avenue of regularly planted Trees Leading to the different Streets running at right Angles toward the River." He wasn't overly impressed: "Main Street . . . as well as the generality of the place [is] too narrow to be Handsome, [and] is rendered Less Interesting by the poorness and Iregularity of the Houses, few of which are Brick — and at this season very much encumbered by Bales of Cotton." He found conveniences, including a hotel ("a good House built on the Spanish plan, e.g. with Large Piazas and Many Doors and Windows"); several taverns; plus "a Bank in good Credit — a Post Office receiving the Diferent Mails Thrice per Week, a Public reading room and 2 printing offices." He reported, too, of "Country back of Natchez . . . represented as Good and fitted by rich planters who [raise] a Large quantity of Cotton the principle article of Export."

Audubon was soon away, back on a flatboat heading for New Orleans. But he would return and spend much of the years 1822 and 1823 in the vicinity. He arranged for his wife to join him, and while she worked as a governess on a nearby plantation, he helped support the family by teaching French, music, drawing, and even dancing in the town. But the arrival of another artist in December 1822 led to his leaving us a second record of Natchez.

The man was John Stein, a now largely forgotten traveling portraitist. The two artists were immediately drawn to one another and became fast friends. Stein proved an important influence on Audubon, giving Audubon his first lessons in the use of oil paints. One of Audubon's apprentice works in oil provides a second, frozen-in-time glimpse of Natchez.

The work on canvas was painted in 1822, and survives as one of the few known landscapes in Audubon's hand. It is a panoramic view of Natchez. A grand house — Clifton, destroyed by Union solders during the Civil War, but a home that Audubon knew — overlooks a town of a few dozen structures. Texada, the early Spanish house in brick, is visible with its hipped roof and dormers. Standing tall are the Adams County Courthouse and the domed Trinity Episcopal Church. In the foreground a small group stands gazing, as well as the artist himself, working beneath a canopy.

Audubon painted a town in the throes of its first prosperity, but there is also much implied in this untitled painting. Its subject is not just what is there but what will soon emerge. The middle distance is open, rolling acreage dotted with grazing cows but no houses. Audubon recorded an odd humped structure on that undeveloped terrain. It was a brick kiln, where the bricks for a soon-to-be constructed house were being fired. When finished the following

John James Audubon's oil painting of Natchez recorded the emerging town as it appeared in 1822.

year, Rosalie would bookend the town, along with Clifton, as if standing guard from the Mississippi banks at the northern and southern limits of the city. In the coming decades, the foreground that Audubon limned as grassy and open would be lined with houses and warehouses, as the growing prosperity enabled Natchezians to build fine homes on an expanding city grid.

In Audubon's landscape, Rosalie is a mere promise. But Peter Little and his wife were in residence there by the following year. And the imposing, columned house, with its Natchez plan, inspired many other fine homes in the city. Audubon moved on; he would never return, although the 435 plates in his monumental *Birds of America* were published between 1828 and 1838. But he left two snapshots — one a written record, the other an apprentice oil painting — that portray Natchez as a place waiting to emerge.

The stairway at Gloucester.

———— ⚬⁄ᴗ ————

By the early nineteenth century, Natchez had gained a reputation as a place to get rich. The melting pot of the early days in the eighteenth century — settlers had come from Spain, France, England, and Scotland — gave way to an American emigration. Some of the new arrivals came on foot along the old Natchez Trace, the longtime Indian trail that meandered south from Nashville, but many of the citizens of the new country made their way to Natchez by water, arriving via the Ohio and Mississippi Rivers. Most were from the North, yet Virginia, perhaps more than any other state, influenced the manner and style of Natchez (as one writer observed, Virginia was Mississippi's "mother country"). The Virginians may have helped set the tone, but the arrivals, whatever their origins, seemed to know what they came for: They wanted to cash in on the cotton boom.

The arrivals brought a new level of education and taste to Natchez. Despite the city's military past and the rough-and-tough riverside settlement at Natchez Under-the-Hill, the surrounding farms began to acquire a more sophisticated air. The new wealth meant people had more time to concern themselves

with matters of style and society, and they wanted new homes that reflected their wealth and aspirations.

Some of these people wanted to show off how much money (and taste) they had, and what better way than by building an impressive home? Back east whence they came, a new generation of architects had begun shaping an American style called Federal in such tastemaking cities as Philadelphia, Baltimore, New York, and Boston. The name isn't very descriptive — it refers to the government of the new nation rather than to the character of the architecture — but the Federal style is indebted to eighteenth-century students of the classical past. Scotsman Robert Adam, Englishman William Chambers, and Americans who included Thomas Jefferson, Charles Bulfinch, and Asher Benjamin were promulgating a refined new manner.

The goal was to provide more than mere shelter: These decorated houses were themselves decorative. Windows, doors, and mantels were capped by moldings, keystones, and pediments. Porch posts gave way to columns. Carved swags, elliptical window frames, and capitals appeared. These were ornamental features based on ancient Roman and Greek models. They were details derived from the essential scheme of architectural classicism. Embodied by a ponderous-sounding doctrine called "the orders," the Classical, Neo-Classical, and Federal styles are, to put it simply, alternative means of combining the prescribed details in the Doric, Ionic, and Corinthian modes with the vertical posts and horizontal beams that constitute the structure of a classical building.

The galleries in Natchez are a fitting symbol of how times were changing. Once a simple affair, little more than a porch with a low-pitched roof to keep off the sun, the gallery was superseded in high-style Natchez houses by grand porticoes with fluted columns and elaborately carved capitals. The talents and tools of millworkers were required rather than the crude on-site implements of the carpenter-builder, who earlier would simply have planed and chamfered a tree trunk. Plain and sturdy was no longer enough; the vernacular had become too commonplace, too lowbrow. The classical had arrived.

Gloucester

Constructed circa 1803
Remodeled 1807 and circa 1830

*G*loucester, at first sight, looks Grecian: Four colossal columns stand proudly forth, a grand expression of its owner's wealth and status. But judging a book by its cover is usually a mistake, and the tall Tuscan portico at Gloucester partly obscures a richer and more complex story.

The columns were raised in the 1830s, when a taste for the Grecian mode became *de rigueur* in Natchez. But the narrative of Gloucester's construction began about three decades earlier when a two-story brick house was built a mile south of the Natchez city limits. Then called Bellevue, the original structure was what we think of today as a classic colonial: two stories tall,

The entrance façade at Gloucester. Note the semi-octagonal shape of the building's end wall.

five bays wide, with a center hall behind its front door. The entrance was the focal design element, with its tall, thin pilasters framing a semicircular fanlight over the door.

In 1807 the property was sold and its new owner promptly renamed it "Gloster Place" in honor of his Massachusetts birthplace. Winthrop Sargent (1753-1820) was a man of accomplishments. He was a Harvard graduate, an honored veteran of the Continental Army, former secretary of the Territory Northwest of the River Ohio, and, between 1798 and 1801, he had been governor of the Mississippi Territory. Though retired from public life, Sargent was still vigorously accumulating enormous agricultural holdings, which included lands not only in Mississippi and Louisiana but in Ohio and Virginia as well. In the next few years, he set about making Gloucester his own in more than name.

The original doorway offers a key clue to the next step in the evolution of the house. It survives intact but, thanks to Sargent's remodeling, no longer stands at the center of the front façade. A second, matching doorway was

Several early dependencies survive intact at Gloucester, including a two-story brick kitchen and slave quarter.

added in order to maintain symmetry. This unusual double-entrance design helps mask the large extension Sargent commissioned for the east end of Gloucester. Including cabinet rooms and galleries added to the rear, Sargent's renovation more than doubled the volume of the original house.

The changes Sargent made, together with the later addition of the front portico, make Gloucester unique. And its rarity grows more apparent on closer examination: The angles of the half-octagon ends of the house don't match (for no evident reason). And there are two stair halls in the main block of the house — not a main and a servants' stair but two stylish principal stairways. Oddities such as these can make a house feel ill-considered or haphazard. Yet at Gloucester the eccentricity helps make the house an important, if individualized, reflection of changing times.

The alignment of doors or enfilade *across the front of Gloucester offers a view from one end of the house to the other through the forty-two-foot-long front passage.*

The current owners at Gloucester have chosen to furnish the dining room (below) with Chippendale-style chairs and the sitting room (left) with comfortable upholstered sofas.

Auburn

Two gentlemen from Massachusetts were responsible for building Auburn. One was the client, Judge Lyman G. Harding, a lawyer who was the Mississippi Territory's first attorney general. The other was the designer-builder, Levi G. Weeks, who had arrived via New York where he'd been tried (and acquitted) for the murder of his fiancée. Both men found the frontier ways of Natchez suited them. Harding made an enormous fortune in the cotton business, while Weeks, his checkered reputation forgotten, got to build what he himself called "the first house in the territory on which was ever attempted any of the orders of architecture."

The thirty-one-foot-tall portico is Auburn's defining characteristic, but prior to the addition of the wings (the pairs of bays at each end), it must have been even more impressive.

Harding purchased open acreage just east of town in 1807, but Weeks described it best. The setting, he wrote to a friend back in Massachusetts, is "one of those peculiar situations which combines all the delight of romance – the pleasures of rurality and the approach of sublimity." In the same letter, written in September 1812, Weeks felt empowered to make claims for his work, too. "The brick house I am building," he wrote, "[will be] the most magnificent building in the Territory."

Auburn would live up to its billing and become a house that influenced the design of countless other antebellum mansions across the South. Weeks created in Auburn one of the first houses in America fronted by a portico with a pedimented (triangular) roof supported by colossal (two-

Left:
The front entrance at Auburn is a particularly skillful conception: surely the inspiration came from a book, but in execution, the practiced hands of Levi Weeks, craftsman, gave it an American Federal feel.

Right:
Auburn's staircase is a tour de force. *Its plan is circular, the structure of steamed and bent wood, and the effect is of a dizzying sculptural presence in the entry hall. Weeks borrowed the design from a 1757 builder's book,* British Palladio *by William Pain.*

story) columns. Auburn's form became a cliché, the Gone-with-the-Wind plantation house standardized. Weeks – and Auburn – announced the coming of columns and cornices.

Weeks introduced something else to Natchez that proved to be just as important. Before his arrival, the norm had been vernacular buildings, planters' cottages, that were adapted to the climate. But Weeks brought a deeper historical consciousness to design. At the time of his death in 1819, his estate included a collection of architectural reference books, and historians have traced many design touches at Auburn – among them the circular stairs and various door architraves – to specific eighteenth-century volumes. Though commonplace in cultural centers in the east, adherence to such historic precedent was new in the Territory. In the decades that followed, however, dozens of other Natchez buildings would incorporate academically correct classical elements based on Renaissance, Roman, and Greek buildings as reproduced in the plates of English and American plan books.

After Harding's death in 1820, Auburn was acquired by a physician and planter, Dr. Stephen Duncan. He added matching wings to the house and a second portico on the rear. A Union sympathizer, Duncan returned to his native Pennsylvania during the Civil War and never came back to Mississippi. A half century later, his descendants donated the house and 210 acres to the city of Natchez.

The drawing room features retarditaire *(old-fashioned) architraves topped by a swan-necked split pediment. As he did with the stairs, Weeks adopted the design from a plate in an eighteenth-century architectural reference.*

Today the site is a city park, and Auburn has a municipal swimming pool and a public golf course in its backyard. The terms of the gift stipulated that the house was to be used for the "amusement, entertainment, and recreation, without cost or monetary consideration, of Natchez citizens," and the city lived up to its commitment. Public meetings were held in Auburn's parlors and children roller skated in the halls. One of Natchez's most influential works of architecture became a community center, and it wasn't until 1972, well after the establishment of the Pilgrimage, that care for the house was given over to the Auburn Garden Club. The club refurbished Auburn and opened it for tours as a house museum.

The family furnishings were auctioned after Dr. Duncan's heirs gifted the house to the city of Natchez in 1911, but a mixture of appropriate objects has been installed in the house, including some returned by Duncan and Harding family members.

Yet the contents are less memorable than the architectural details. In 1812, much of the work might have seemed old-fashioned in a trendier place than Natchez, but the city was then perched at the edge of the civilized world. Weeks's use of Georgian elements from decades-old books probably seemed fresh to Harding and other Natchezians. But Weeks, as he said he would do, put the "the orders of Architecture" on display, using Ionic columns and a Corinthian entablature on his portico. And he didn't limit himself solely to printed plates, but roamed freely, borrowing and adapting. His manner would be much admired – and imitated – in the years to come.

Linden

CONSTRUCTED CIRCA 1815
REMODELED AFTER 1835

As the fortunes of Natchez expanded, so did the need for impressive houses. Thomas Reed had lived on the property for some years when he purchased the land in 1818, and very likely he had built the house in which he resided. The dwelling consisted of two rooms and a central passage on each of two stories, and much of that structure survives at the core of Linden. The portico to Reed's house gave it immediate prominence – just as Reed himself would soon become Senator Reed, representing Mississippi in the United States Senate.

Though the portico and the colonnades were the result of two different building campaigns, Linden's façade seems to welcome the visitor with open arms.

The rear of the house is flanked by two wings that were added piecemeal in the decades before the Civil War.

The next owner, Dr. John Ker, added two matching wings and an ell after Reed's death in 1829, producing a house that closely resembles the structure that stands today. Ker also gave the place its current name, Linden.

The unmistakable character of Linden is not a matter of its geometric parts. Rather, as one architectural historian has written, Linden "is ordinary in form but extraordinary in detail." And those details bring the building to life. This house lacks the classical rigor of Auburn – there's a country-boy quality to the way the disparate boxy shapes come together. But Reed's builders executed the individual parts masterfully in the Federal style, including the carved mantels, a sunburst window in the pediment, and the entrance with its sidelights, transom fanlight, and columns. Greek Revival elements survive from the Ker ownership, among them the turned balusters that line the upper gallery.

Over Linden's dining room table hangs a fine example of a Natchez punkah. Also known as a "shoo-fly," the punkah is a large wooden fan, usually operated by a slave, that was swung by pulling a rope that operated a system of pulleys.

The house is on the outskirts of Natchez, and visitors today, whether on Pilgrimage tours or as bed-and-breakfast guests, see a home that is prototypical Natchez. Some of its elements suggest frontier days and the residual Spanish influence, but most came later. The house grew over time. The ceilings got higher, the windowpanes larger, and the decorations more elaborate. It has now been home to the same family for six generations (since the first Connor acquired the property in 1849). At Linden — as in so much of Natchez — there is a lingering sense of both continuity and change.

Rosalie

CONSTRUCTED 1821-1823 AND AFTER

*R*osalie has a storybook look — *and* the stories to match. The first tale tells of an orphaned girl and her principled guardian who, in the end, married and lived happily ever after. Another tells of a great shopping spree. It took place in New York in 1858, but the result is a decorative-arts time capsule at Rosalie today. Then there's the encampment of the conquering generals (and, no, they didn't wreck the place but behaved like perfect gentlemen). All of these historical moments add texture to the history of a remarkable house that, along with Auburn, influenced a thousand other fine plantation houses across the South.

The front façade of Peter Little's Rosalie.

While its tall portico may lack the academic accuracy of Auburn's, Rosalie's makes an even bolder statement in its setting overlooking the Mississippi River.

The guardian in the first story was one Peter Little, who purchased twenty-two acres on the Natchez bluff in 1821. The land had been the parade grounds of the original French settlement at Fort Rosalie, with a panoramic vista of the Mississippi River. Little had come to Natchez in 1798 at the age of seventeen seeking his fortune. He became both a planter and a sawmill operator, producing building materials at a time when construction was booming (in 1818 he would open the first steam-powered sawmill on the river). His prosperity enabled him to build the fine house that is Rosalie.

His motivation for doing so probably came from the orphaned girl, Eliza Ann Lowe. As a young man, Little had taken frequent ferry trips back and forth to his Concordia Parish properties in Louisiana. He had become fast friends with the ferryman, Jacob Lowe. When Lowe and his wife both died suddenly in 1806 of yellow fever, Little was entrusted with a young ward. According to territorial law, Eliza was unable to inherit her father's property as a minor child, but Little came up with a

The rear galleries extend the full width of Rosalie. Food for the table was brought by slaves from a detached dependency and served through a ground-floor window.

solution. He quickly married the thirteen-year-old girl but, as a man of propriety, he promptly shipped her back to his native Maryland, where she was educated in fashionable Baltimore. She rejoined him in Natchez several years later and they began their lives as man and wife. By all accounts, they lived happily at Rosalie until Eliza fell victim to "Yellow Jack," as her parents had done, and died in 1853. Peter Little died three years later.

The architecture of Rosalie is engaging, even without reference to its eventful past. The design may have been the work of Little's brother-in-law, James Shryock Griffin of Baltimore. The tall building isn't quite a cube but resembles one, standing on its raised basement and almost square footprint (fifty-six-feet wide by sixty-five deep). Its

Two bedrooms at Rosalie, one with a half-tester bed (opposite left), the other with a youth bed covered with protective mosquito netting.

impressive bulk is topped by a hipped roof and a widow's walk. The rear elevation of the house is lined with six more colossal columns that front a deep double gallery. This combination of forms – a cubical block, fronted by a portico and backed by two-story galleries – would prove an enduring form. It would be revived with minor modifications many times later at Natchez (in such landmarks as Magnolia Hall, Melrose, and Stanton Hall) as well as elsewhere in the lower Mississippi valley and across the South. Inside the scale of the ten rooms is just as impressive, with thirteen-

foot ceilings, and a deep double parlor.

The exterior of Rosalie remains largely as constructed, but the interior saw a modest up-dating after the deaths of Peter and Eliza Little. Andrew L. Wilson, a transplanted Pennsylvanian grown rich as a cotton broker, purchased the house in 1857. He and his wife promptly refurbished the interior. Their remodeling involved some changes in architectural fabric, with new plaster ceiling medallions and updated marble mantels that replaced the earlier wooden Federal ones. The result was a suitable setting for the Victorian furniture they purchased on a shopping trip to New York the following year.

Among the objects the Wilsons purchased were gilt overmantel mirrors. Natchez legend has it that less than five years after installing them, the Wilsons found themselves removing the mirrors, wrapping them in cotton, and burying them in the backyard. Much other furniture is said to have been consigned to the attic, all in anticipation of

The Wilsons furnished the double parlor with new marble mantels, Brussels carpets, gilt mirrors, and, most memorably, twenty-one pieces of Rococo Revival furniture from the workshop of New York maker John Henry Belter.

the arrival of Yankee troops. Rosalie was subsequently occupied by Union forces, with the main floor functioning as offices and mess hall; living quarters for General and Mrs. Walter Q. Gresham were established upstairs, along with Mrs. Wilson and her daughter (Andrew Wilson had fled to Texas). Despite being the head of an occupying force, Gresham is remembered warmly in Natchez as a gracious and considerate guest.

Rosalie remained in the Wilson family after the war, but went into the public trust in 1938 when it was purchased from Wilson descendants by the Mississippi State Society of the Daughters of the American Revolution. Even then, however, the house came complete not only with Wilson objects but also with two tenants. With the death of the last of the Wilson heirs in 1958, the storied Rosalie ceased being a residence and formally became the historic site it is today.

Hawthorne

CONSTRUCTED CIRCA 1825

Appearances can be deceptive, and Hawthorne is an architectural example. Its front façade has the hallmark of a planter's house, the deep gallery supported by six boxed piers. Yet Hawthorne is believed to have been constructed well after the territorial period, probably about 1825. In fact, the porch itself dates from even later, perhaps the 1840s or even 1850s. Hawthorne, in short, is not what it seems.

A glance beneath the porch offers a hint of the real story. There's an elegantly executed Federal fan sash over the front entrance, with matching sidelights and pilasters. Inside the house there are no fewer than three

The unassuming face of Hawthorne. The dormers were added in the twentieth century.

more such fan sashes, two of which are set into walls adjacent to the front entrance and look into the parlor and dining room to either side. Belying its cottagelike exterior, Hawthorne's interior is surprisingly grand, with high ceilings and a generous center hall.

Hawthorne may be characterized as "trickle-down" Federal, with stylish craftsmanship on the inside but an unprepossessing and relaxed exterior. Unlike Lyman Harding at Auburn or Peter Little at Rosalie, Hawthorne's owners weren't aiming to make a grand statement to approaching visitors. The scale of the house is modest, standing one-and-a-half stories tall, and it is only after being welcomed inside Hawthorne that its generous proportions and fine details are evident.

The central hall or passage at Hawthorne (opposite left) no longer opens to the outdoors at the front and the back, as a modern family room has been added at the rear of the house (above). An open gallery was enclosed and now provides a large and comfortable place for the family and guests to gather.

Dunleith's columns march around all four sides of its square footprint.

CHAPTER 3

The Grecian Mode

RICHMOND
THE BURN
D'EVEREUX
GREEN LEAVES
COTTAGE GARDENS
CHEROKEE
MELROSE
LANSDOWNE
MONMOUTH
DUNLEITH

"[Natchez is] the largest town of the State of Mississippi, containing . . . many handsome houses . . . [and] delightful views . . . . [O]ne of the most beautiful towns in the United States."
James Stuart, *Three Years in North America*, 1833

"The Agricultural bank," wrote Joseph Holt Ingraham, "is unquestionably the finest structure in the city." The soon-to-be author (his first book, *The South-West by a Yankee*, would be published in 1835) arrived in Natchez just in time to see the completed building, which had been constructed in 1833. He raved about the bank, describing its exterior as "presenting a noble colonnaded front, of the modernized Grecian style" and the "vast hall" inside as "decidedly the finest room south or west of Washington."

Ingraham brought a fresh eye to the city of Natchez. Born into a well-to-do Maine shipping family, he was able to pursue a youthful desire to see the world. He traveled down the Mississippi, disembarked at Natchez, and spent some months getting acquainted. He described the main street as "compactly built with handsome brick blocks," but he was more impressed by the activity of the place. "The stranger is struck with the extraordinary number of private carriages, clustered before the doors of the most fashionable stores."

The Grecian Mode

"Few of these equipages are of the city," he continued. "They are from the plantations in the neighborhood, which spread out from the town." Given the opportunity to visit not a few of these homes, he wasn't overly impressed. The grounds he termed "neglected" and "unornamented," with little shrubbery or "other artificial auxiliaries to the natural scenery." Inside the homes, he observed, "Many of the wealthiest planters are lodged wretchedly [with] a splendid sideboard not unfrequently concealing a white-washed beam – a gorgeous Brussels carpet laid over a rough-planked floor – while uncouth rafters, in ludicrous contrast to the splendour they look down upon, stretch in coarse relief across the ceiling."

In the decades to come, Ingraham would become a prolific author of romances, but even as a young man he recognized a story unfolding. He saw an explanation for the fancy furnishings ("carpets, elegant furniture, costly mantel ornaments, and side-boards loaded with massive plate") found in unfancy dwellings. "These discrepancies," he wrote, "always characteristic of a new country, are rapidly disappearing; and another generation will be lodged, if not like princes, at least, like independent American gentlemen."

He was at least half right. The next generation would indeed have more stylish accommodations – though not a few of them would prove so extravagant as to be almost princely. And many would be "noble" and "colonnaded" and "Grecian" like the Agricultural Bank he so admired.

For a consciously fashionable place, Natchez took its time in adopting the vogue for Grecian architecture. The style had seen its American introduction in Philadelphia with the Bank of Pennsylvania (1798) and gradually moved to other East Coast cities like Boston and Baltimore where, by the close of the 1820s, it had become *the* new style. In Natchez the building that aroused Ingraham's admiration, the Agricultural Bank of Natchez, launched the Greek Revival a bit later, in 1833.

Once it arrived, however, the Grecian style became the mode of the moment. The Burn and D'Evereux, both completed in about 1836, represent two of its early manifestations (see pages 101 and 105, respectively). The Burn is a relatively modest house, a recognizable heir to the planter's cottage. But D'Evereux is grand indeed, with great piers supporting a deep, two-story porch. It's a classic plantation house of the sort that many people associate with life in the South before the Civil War. Many other houses rose in the years that followed, including the grand and pristine Grecian statement Melrose (page 131) and more modest cottage variations like Lansdowne (page 137) and Cottage Gardens (page 117). A number of other houses were renovated in the Grecian style, as homes like Richmond and Cherokee were updated (see pages 93 and 123). In the quarter-century before the outbreak of the Civil War, Natchez would acquire a new and distinctly Grecian look.

When it was constructed in 1833, the Agricultural Bank of Natchez on Main Street was the first Grecian building in town. It would prove to be the first of many in the Greek Revival style. Collection of Thomas H. Gandy and Joan W. Gandy.

Richmond

CONSTRUCTED CIRCA 1784
REMODELED CIRCA 1832 AND 1860

*T*o walk through Richmond is to see the story of Natchez in architectural terms.

In about 1784 the first structure at Richmond was built. It consisted of a simple wooden cottage, a story and a half tall, set atop an enclosed service floor. In the next few years — the precise dates are unknown — galleried porches were applied to the front and back of the house. Federal moldings and other decorative touches were added in another, superficial remodeling. In short, the place assumed the look of numerous other Mississippi planters' houses in the early years of the nineteenth century.

In a careful exercise in the Grecian manner, Levin Marshall added this new section to an earlier house in 1832.

The 1832 addition to Richmond became the front of the house; in 1860 a second addition of brick was attached to the rear. Sandwiched in between is the much modified original structure dating from the late eighteenth century.

The second major construction phase began when a Virginian named Levin R. Marshall purchased the house in 1832. Marshall had arrived in Mississippi at seventeen. Having married well and demonstrated a considerable business acumen as a banker, he wanted a house that proclaimed his rising status. He added an entirely new structure to one end of Richmond, a tall and impressive block built in the new Grecian style. In the coming decades Marshall would invest in hotels and steamships, and amass immense agricultural holdings. His ambitions were large, and the classical detailing of the addition suggests something of his desire to do things correctly. The two pairs of fluted columns on the portico are Ionic; the entrance it protects is in the elaborate Corinthian order; the façade is capped with a parapet of turned balusters.

This is a statement house — it proclaims not only wealth but taste.

Just before the Civil War, the third and final construction phase added a tall brick addition at the opposite end of the original cottage. This hip-roofed structure enclosed six bedrooms and, in the way that life sometimes echoes art, it proved a harbinger for the subsequent history of the house — and, in a sense, of Natchez itself. Very little has changed at Richmond since the 1860 addition was built, not even the ownership. It has passed seamlessly from one generation of heirs to the next, and today is jointly owned by four of Levin Marshall's great-great-great-grandchildren. As caretakers, they have assumed responsibility not only for a magnificent house, but one filled with furniture, objects, and interior details.

From the inside looking out — note the Corinthian capitals with the carved acanthus leaves and the Ionic capitals with the scrolls or volutes.

In particular, the circa 1832 Grecian portion of the house conveys a sense of Levin Marshall's aspirations. Its form is commonplace — it's a rudimentary five-bay, double-pile house. The five openings across the front look into two rooms on either side that flank the central stair hall. As a result, it isn't the mass or the volumes that make the place memorable — it's the finish. Inside as well as out the self-conscious display of architectural detail defines it: Pilasters line the parlor walls as if to allude to the central hall in an ancient house. There are massive architraves, and classical orders abound.

This is one of those houses that has never been restored — restoration isn't necessary when little or nothing has ever been taken away. As one of its owners recently remarked, "I can't think"— she paused, thinking deeply — "no, I can't think of one thing that is not in the same place as it was when I was a child."

The walls of this front parlor are lined with pilasters (flattened columns). The piano was used to accompany the singing of Jenny Lind, "the Swedish nightingale," on her visit to Natchez.

Opposite right:
One of two dining rooms at Richmond, furnished just as it was in Levin Marshall's time.

Right:
Call it a "bathing room," if you wish — that's an early shower, one of a collection of early bathroom fixtures at Richmond.

Below:
The main passage in the Grecian addition to Richmond, with the earliest section of the house visible through the doorway beneath the stairs.

The Grecian Mode

The Burn

CONSTRUCTED CIRCA 1836

John P. Walworth set off to make his fortune. Leaving his birthplace in Aurora, New York, his first stop was Cleveland, but the urge for going soon struck again. So the twenty-one year old Walworth boarded a steamship, with New Orleans as his destination. Little did he realize when he disembarked en route for a brief look around Natchez that he would live out his days there.

Upon his arrival in 1819, he found work as a postal clerk. He married the postmaster's daughter and, in the coming years, became a merchant, banker, plantation owner, and even mayor of Natchez. But it was in 1836 that he commissioned construction of The Burn, a house that says a good deal about the man.

The Burn may resemble a little house in the country — in fact, it's a large house surrounded by other houses within the Natchez city limits.

The gable end of the house reveals its true scale — and three stories of living space.

The house was probably designed by T.J. Hoyt, but whoever drew the plans knew what was *au courant*, as The Burn was one of the first houses in Natchez built in the new Grecian style. Certainly Walworth had the means to build whatever he wished, but he chose to incorporate the opulent architectural details on the inside of his new house. The exterior isn't showy: It is set back from the street and appears to be a story-and-a-half tall (in fact, another full basement story is disguised by the small rise into which the house was constructed). Walworth's house seems somehow cautious, the domicile of a reserved man who kept his own counsel and felt no need to display his wealth. Of Scots descent, Walworth named his new home The Burn, after the brook (or "burn" or "bourn") that meandered across his hundred-acre estate.

The front façade is dominated by the portico – a conscious echo of the Greek temple – with its bold Doric details, wide band of horizontal trim (entablature), and large half-round window in the pediment above. Upon entering through the elaborate doorway with its fluted columns, the visitor is immediately struck by the curving staircase that appears suspended in the hall directly ahead. Many of the details in the house, including mantels, doors, and window architraves have the unmistakable bulk and strength of Greek Revival detailing.

An original dependency extends to the rear. The house has seen a variety of uses since construction, having been commandeered by Union forces during the Civil War for use as a hospital. It was returned to residential use after the war and John Walworth's heirs resided in the home until 1935; more recently The Burn has served as a bed-and-breakfast accommodation and a stop on the Pilgrimage tour.

Above:
The dramatic semicircular staircase in the central hall at The Burn.

Below:
At The Burn, the parlor in the foreground is divided from the dining room to the rear by a boldly trimmed double doorway.

D'Evereux

Constructed 1836

Quite by chance, D'Evereux is symbolic of two Natchez transitions. In architectural style, the house is Grecian at its most impressive, despite discernible vestiges of the Federal style that had just become passé; and its setting, once an eighty-acre preserve on the outskirts of Natchez, has shrunk to seven acres abutting a four-lane highway. Thus D'Evereux (*DEV-rue*) represents the city both as it approached its acme and as it has adapted to modern times.

This big, bold house was built for William St. John Elliott, a Maryland-born planter and president of the Natchez Protection Insurance

The sheer size of the elements is what is most striking about the front façade of D'Evereux with its row of six fluted, twenty-four-foot-tall Doric columns.

Among the parlor furnishings at D'Evereux is a gilt-legged Rococo piano. Though not original to the house, the ornate piece fits its bold scale and brash confidence.

Company. His wealth enabled Elliott to commission a monumental edifice. D'Evereux has an austere grandeur, its stark white block topped by a low hip roof and cupola. The property was named after St. John Elliott's maternal uncle, General John D'Evereux, who had served with South American liberator Simón Bolívar.

On the interior, the details of the house emerge, with fine plaster moldings decorating the ceilings and bold Grecian door and window architraves. The scale of the interior remains outsized, but there is a feeling of warm hospitality at D'Evereux, as at so many of the homes of Natchez. While the place was clearly designed to remind visitors of the depth of Elliott's pockets, it was also as a place for entertaining, for society and sociability.

The house had its dark days, as it served as barracks for Union troops during the Civil War. In the years after, tenant farmers resided in the house, and some rooms were even used to store crops. Then in 1925 a school-teacher from Chicago acquired the home and, though its property has been subdivided (in 1962 a Baptist church acquired the bulk of the eighty acres), D'Evereux has been treated respectfully by subsequent inhabitants.

The Grecian Mode

Above:
At D'Evereux, as in many Natchez mansions, the central passages are more than hallways, and are large and grand enough for use as living spaces.

Left:
Mature plantings and a surviving dependency (left) define the gracious garden in the rear yard at D'Evereux.

Green Leaves

CONSTRUCTED 1838

The sense of continuity at Green Leaves is palpable. Just inside the entrance, the visitor may examine a sequence of antique portraits. Upon walking deeper into the house, the paintings on canvas are succeeded by a series of photographic portraits. Initially a girl in a prom dress seems to have little to connect her to the countenance of an old settler, but gradually the realization sinks in: A short walk down the central hall at Green Leaves amounts to a century-and-a-half journey along the trunk of a family tree.

There's a child's dress on display that was worn at the first pilgrimage in 1932. When the lady of the house tells its story, it emerges that it was

When viewed from Wall Street, Green Leaves has modest curb appeal, a substantial but understated dwelling.

The child in the foreground of this 1932 photograph is Virginia Beltzhoover Morrison who, decades later, opens her house just as her mother (left) did in the early days of the Pilgrimage. Collection of Thomas H. Gandy and Joan W. Gandy.

she who wore that gown seventy-odd years ago. Other gowns that appear in some of the pictures have been carefully displayed nearby. The house is full of wedding presents – from weddings that took place generations ago. If the people who have lived here didn't save everything, they certainly saved a lot of the right objects.

The significance of Green Leaves isn't especially apparent on first approach. The house is only one story tall and originally was only two rooms deep. It sits on a half-block lot of the city grid, slightly elevated above the downtown street, partly obscured by a screen of flowering azaleas and camellias. A post-and-lintel portico stands front and center: Though richly detailed with triglyphs on its frieze and fluted columns, it's a modestly proportioned entrance porch. The academically correct architectural details are there for those who look, but the effect is not so much ornamented as of simple elegance.

Museums aspire to the condition of Green Leaves: Virtually everything in these double parlors is original to the antebellum era of George Washington Koontz.

The home was constructed in 1838 by a developer, Edward P. Fourniquet, but the house today is a memorial to George Washington Koontz and his descendants. A Pennsylvanian who arrived in Natchez in 1836, he was a partner in the Britton and Koontz Bank. The understated exterior of the place appealed to his bankerly reserve; he chose to show off indoors where the sense of restraint quickly disappears.

The interior moldings and millwork are among the most ornamented of any residence in town. There are deep overhanging cornices, tall and generous doorways, and many Grecian details. But for the student of decorative arts, this is mere stage dressing, as original treatments abound on floors, walls, and windows. In the double drawing room there is an assemblage of original materials, including wallpapers, rugs, portieres, and curtains. Among the furnishings bought for the house that survive is carved furniture in the Empire and Rococo Revival styles, as well as richly veined black marble mantels and ornate gilt over-mantel mirrors.

Green Leaves offers living history in the best sense — yes, some of the other hostesses at Pilgrimage don costumes, too, but here it's more than that. The owners of this house have recognized they own a remarkably unspoiled and invaluable survivor from another time. It's become more important than one person; the property is now owned by a family trust concerned with its preservation. The result is that Green Leaves is a home that throws open its doors to guests for a time before closing them and returning, once again, to the normal everyday habitation of a fine house that generations of George Koontz's children and grandchildren have called home. It's a place where a single room contains china said to have been painted by John James Audubon and, a short distance away on a bedside table, a sign of our times, sits a telephone. Despite the quality of the collections, Green Leaves is the opposite of a museum.

Above right:
The rear of the house evolved over time, with a three-bed-room wing added in the 1850s and, late in the nineteenth century, the brick dependency facing it. The house seems to embrace the rear courtyard shaded by an aged live oak.

Right:
The woodwork, the fabrics, the papers — even the parlor games set out on the table have been in situ at Green Leaves for many decades.

The Grecian Mode

Left:
The biggest single change from generation to generation seems to be the addition of more objects, in particular paintings and photographs of members of the family. The house and its inhabitants are inextricably linked.

Cottage Gardens

Constructed circa 1840

The name suits this modest-seeming house amid its generous lot and lush plantings. The original structure on what was then a large land grant may have begun as home to the last of the Spanish governors, but today's one-and-a-half-story structure assumed its present form much later, probably before 1840. And the name came later still, after the property changed hands in 1884.

The full-width porch or gallery, so typical of earlier Natchez houses, survives here beneath a triangular pediment. The original squared-off log columns were replaced in the 1960s with round columns, giving the house a

Though not original to the house (the room was redesigned in the 1960s by New Orleans architect A. Hays Town), the finish of the library with its bold pilasters, built-in shelves and cupboards, and overmantel paneling suits the house and its impressive collections.

Top: From the street, Cottage Gardens and its plantings have a deceptively simple look.

more formal quality that suits the stylish elliptical window above. Rather like The Burn barely a block away — which may well have been designed by the same man, T.J. Hoyt — this is a wood-frame house that on approach looks humbler than it is, since its interior was outfitted with such fine architectural details, including a dramatic curving staircase.

The current owners decided the careful symmetry and generous proportions of the rooms would make Cottage Gardens an excellent backdrop for their passion for collecting, which had outgrown their previous residence. The eighteenth-century Irish and American furniture they collect predates Cottage Gardens and the great days of Natchez. Yet the fine examples of Philadelphia and Dublin craftsmanship suit the scale of the rooms and are shown to advantage against the simple architectonics of the Grecian moldings.

Above and left: Behind Cottage Gardens, an elaborate walled garden has been constructed with elaborate plantings, a fountain, and a raised seating area atop matching curved staircases.

Right:
The curved staircase in the central hall at Cottage Gardens, along with an Irish side table (right) dating from about 1750. The table is richly carved mahogany with a satyr's mask at the center of its skirt.

Far right:
The peaceful front porch at Cottage Gardens with its sturdy columns and delicate railing.

Below:
In the parlor at Cottage Gardens are pieces of high-style colonial-era furniture, including an English George II settee, a Philadelphia Chippendale drop-front desk, and a Philadelphia high chest of drawers (highboy).

Below right:
In the dining room, the chairs are English from the reign of George III and the chest-on-chest was made in Philadelphia, circa 1765.

Cherokee

Cherokee is a charming little mystery. The lot on which the house stands today changed hands in 1794 and again in 1799, but the construction date of the first house remains unknown. Records suggest that a frame house stood on the site by 1805, and other evidence indicates that the structure was remodeled sometime about 1810. The uncertainty continues: In the mid-1830s (perhaps 1834 or 1835 or 1836?) a house that resembles today's Cherokee began to emerge from an extensive Grecian remodeling that left virtually no sign of the earlier structure.

Cherokee stands apart from its neighbors, with a high-and-mighty air atop its rise, a hillock contained by brick retaining walls.

Above:
The garden at the rear of Cherokee cannot be seen from the street, so its central fountain and lush plantings are a happy surprise to the visitor.

Right:
It is a classic Greek Revival entrance, with paneled pilasters, sidelights, and tall transoms, but with a difference: The faux finishes at Cherokee's entrance are dramatic, featuring a grain-painted door and stucco walling painted to look like cut stone mortared in place.

A powerful 1840 tornado did extensive damage to the new house, but it, too, was rebuilt, though probably not until the middle of the decade.

The site gives Cherokee particular distinction. The setting is indisputably in-town, just blocks from the river and the center of the business district — but upon approach, Cherokee has an almost

fortified feel, since gated stairs must be climbed to reach the front door. The effect is to separate the place from the hustle-bustle of the city streets.

If at first Cherokee seems unapproachable, it has a welcoming quality up close. Its Grecian face is reserved, its entrance porch recessed behind Doric columns. The exterior is of stuccoed brick that recently had its original faux finish restored, giving it the look of a house built of ashlar block. The sight lines from the house are well above the street, offering a bird's-eye view of the surrounding streetscape.

The grand dining room at Cherokee, overlooking the street below.

The details are high-style Grecian, with much carving, and bold transoms and sidelights at the front that light the large parlor that is at the core of the house just inside. The house gradually reveals itself as larger than it appears, with bedrooms above, a lower story below, and formal gardens behind. However and whenever the house we see today was built, Cherokee was worth waiting for.

Above:
A comfortable guest chamber at Cherokee.

Right:
Looking back to the front of the house from the parlor, the entry is at center and the dining room (left) and a private sitting room (right) can be glimpsed.

Melrose

CONSTRUCTED 1845-1847

*A*uthors of architectural style books seek prototypes. They look for models of stylistic purity, for buildings that display the standard forms and details of a given style. Melrose offers just such a paradigm: It is a textbook example of the Greek Revival (or Grecian) style.

The entrance porch is an undisguised Greek temple. In architectural argot it's a tetrastyle (four-columned) portico incorporating Doric columns that are topped by a horizontal band of moldings (the entablature) and a triangular pediment. The details are correct, but the surfaces are not ornate. Unlike the earlier Federal style, the Grecian involved less surface decoration and more pure geometric shapes. For an observer standing at a distance or at

Melrose amid the eighty acres of its parklike setting.

Right:
The front portico at Melrose, an imposing exercise in scale and simplicity.

Below:
The rear of the house, in contrast to its austere and uncomplicated façade, looks into a courtyard enclosed on three sides by the galleries that line the back of the house as well as the two symmetrically placed dependencies. The scale there is monumental, too, with great square piers supporting the porches.

Melrose's doorstep, the message of Melrose is one of permanence and power.

That was exactly what Americans of the era aspired to, among them John T. McMurran. McMurran, born in Pennsylvania and trained as an attorney in Ohio, came to Natchez and became a partner with John A. Quitman, later a Mississippi governor. McMurran married into wealth, and he and his wife, Mary Louisa, purchased 133 suburban acres, surrounded by such properties as Auburn, Linden, and Quitman's own Monmouth, to build a new and more elaborate home. They commissioned Maryland-born Jacob Byers to design and construct what a writer of one of Byers' obituaries would later call "the palace mansion of J.T. McMurran, Esq." The McMurrans called it Melrose, borrowing the name from a Scots ruin mystically evoked in Sir Walter Scott's romantic poem *The Lay of the Last Minstrel.*

Left:
Melrose's dining room: the table is set
for ten but has space for many more.
The chairs belonged to the
McMurrans, who are thought to have
purchased them in Philadelphia.

Melrose is impressive inside as well as out. This is a fifteen-thousand-square-foot house, with an enormous central hall, a set of three parlors that run the entire length of one side of the house, as well as a grand dining room on the first floor. Upstairs are six bedrooms and another capacious hall. The details throughout are boldly ordered and architectural, with Grecian pilasters, columns, and marble mantels.

The McMurrans spent almost twenty years in the house, but after a series of family tragedies they sold it, together with most of its furnishings, in 1865. It was an on-again, off-again home until 1900 when George M.D. Kelly, a New Yorker who had inherited Melrose and several other Natchez properties, came to tour his holdings with his new

Melrose

The triple parlors at Melrose, chockablock with original furniture.

bride, Ethel. They were destined to make Melrose their full-time residence, and Ethel Moore Kelly lived there until her death in 1975 at the age of ninety-seven. Since 1990 the house has been a museum under the stewardship of the National Park Service.

Despite changes in ownership, the furnishings and finishes at Melrose have remained largely original. A comparison of the contents of the house today with the McMurran inventory of 1865 reveals that Rococo Revival furniture from New York, Philadelphia chandeliers from Cornelius and Company, and a range of decorative objects – paintings, glassware, and

The Grecian Mode

Melrose is a big house, with enormous rooms, and much original furniture to match. This full-tester bed would look badly out of scale in — or wouldn't even fit into — the average twenty-first-century bedroom.

statues — all remain *in situ*. An especially rare vestige is the canvas floorcloth in the central hall. It was block-printed to resemble Brussels woven carpet.

As the central museum holding in the Natchez National Historical Park, the Melrose site, with the main house and its dependencies, provides the opportunity to look at life not only as it was lived by the wealthy planters, but by the slaves who waited upon them.

Lansdowne

CONSTRUCTED 1853

*R*estoration is one thing, preservation another. When a house is restored, elements are recreated, missing parts are put back into place. On the other hand, preservation doesn't involve replacement; rather, it is a matter of cherishing, of retaining, of holding fast to the good elements from the past and ensuring their stability and survival. Preservation of an instinctive kind has been practiced at Lansdowne for a good long time, and the result is an unusual sense of suspended animation.

The house isn't as large as some of the notable mansions in Natchez, standing just one story tall. The house retains its original floor plan, consisting of six rooms plus the central passage. The three rooms extending front-to-back to the right are bedrooms, while across the hall are a generous parlor,

Set amid dense plantings, Lansdowne has the aura of a cottage dwarfed by mature trees.

The wall covering is French, with Zuber figures on a background of Delicourt foliage paper, dating from 1853; the mantel is Italian Carrara marble; the over-mantel mirror was made in America, in the style of the English tastemaker Charles Locke Eastlake. The furniture is rosewood, the gasoliers (now electrified) came from the Philadelphia firm of Cornelius and Baker. Lansdowne's parlor is an intact essay in the decorative arts of the mid-nineteenth century.

dining room, and pantry. Given its modest appearance on the exterior, the scale of the rooms is surprisingly generous. The broad central hall itself is sixty-five feet deep, and the structure is sixty feet wide — meaning that Lansdowne's footprint contains almost four thousand square feet of living space.

Dimensions, however, convey little about this house. The architectural style at Lansdowne is unmistakably Grecian. The front portico has fluted Doric columns, the doorway has engaged columns, sidelights, and a heavy headpiece. Inside there are pilastered doorways, bold molding profiles, and plasterwork cornices and ceiling medal-

Left:
Lansdowne — as this 1930s image of its parlor suggests — is a place where the rule is constancy, not change.
Collection of Thomas H. Gandy and Joan W. Gandy.

Below:
That's a portrait of the original George M. Marshall. He appears to be surveying the dining room from his post over the mantel — and were he to come back to life, he would almost certainly recognize most of the furniture, the silver, and many other objects in the room.

lions. Again, though, Lansdowne's uniqueness isn't a function of its architectural finish.

The lost-in-time quality of Lansdowne is particularly potent because so little has been changed. Along with certain other houses in Natchez, among them Richmond (see page 93) and Green Leaves (page 111), Lansdowne has an unexcavated feel. No one has scratched its surface too deeply meaning that the original Zuber wallpaper lines the walls and the windows are trimmed with precise copies of the original brocaded damask lambrequins. The lavish

The Grecian Mode

The central passage at Lansdowne, lined with generations of family portraits.

decorations include a fine Rococo pierce-carved parlor set. The grain-painting and marbleizing on the woodwork is scratched, some of the fabrics are tattered, and the wallpaper is faded, but the decorating scheme remains intact.

Given the solemn sense of commitment at Lansdowne, perhaps it's appropriate that the property was a wedding gift. The groom, George M. Marshall, had grown up at Richmond; the father of the bride, a wealthy planter, presented some 700 acres three miles north of town to Marshall and his daughter, Charlotte. They then commissioned their brick house, covered with stucco scored to resemble blocks of cut stone. Charlotte's confrontation with Union looters has become part of Natchez legend, as her face was said to have been permanently scarred by a blow delivered by one of the soldiers. The house she sought to protect remains little changed, its hall lined with family portraits, some of which depict the present inhabitants and their children, as Lansdowne has remained the home of George M. Marshall's heirs, including George M. Marshall IV.

A Lansdowne bedroom, with matching tester (canopy) bed and armoire.

Monmouth

CONSTRUCTED 1818
REMODELED 1854

*S*ubtle is not a word that comes to mind when looking at Monmouth. The stark contrast of the lights and darks on the exterior commands your attention, its beige stucco relieved only by dark green blinds. This house has all the assertiveness and confidence of the man responsible for its appearance, John A. Quitman.

A native New Yorker who came to Natchez to make his fortune, Quitman once ran for vice president of the United States. Though he lost that election, his life seems to have been filled with other victories. He was a congressman in Washington and a governor of Mississippi. He won acclaim

Monmouth's stolid portico thrusts forth, supported not by softening columns but by square piers without entasis (taper).

The Zuber wallpaper in the main passage at Monmouth features romanticized American scenes.

and the rank of major general as a war hero in the Mexican War. He was a lawyer and president of a railroad, and a successful planter who owned thousands of acres of cotton and sugar plantations and hundreds of slaves. His investment in the status quo also led him to oppose any compromise on slavery, making him a firm advocate of seccession and states rights in the years before the Civil War.

His house began as a less emphatic statement. At the time of its original construction in 1818, it was a red-brick Federal, built for John Hankinson. He named the house after his birthplace, Monmouth, New Jersey. Vestiges of his house survive inside with doorways that feature elongated, fluted pilasters and fanlights, as well as upstairs mantels with Adamesque fans and the elliptical decorations called *paterae*. The countenance of this house, however, was radically changed after the deaths of the entire Hankinson family in a yellow fever epidemic and Quitman's purchase of the house in 1826.

John Quitman had resided at Monmouth for nearly thirty years when, in 1854, he hired builder James McClure to update his house. McClure elected not to try to compete with the delicate Federal details of the original structure; he took a

more geometric approach, adding the portico, back galleries, and a wing to the rear that gave the footprint an L-shape. Black marble mantels and other elements added an updated feel. Monmouth has become a Natchez icon, a house whose bulky building-block pieces fit together so nicely as to make their assembly look easy. The appeal of Monmouth lies in McClure's carefully calculated balance, symmetry, and proportions, as well as the subliminal impact of the bold lines of the Grecian mode.

Quitman himself died in 1858, but the house remained with his heirs into the early twentieth century. Several changes in title later, the present owners purchased the house and twenty-six acres in 1978 and began its transformation into a sophisticated lodging. Today's Monmouth offers not only bed-and-breakfast accommodations but meeting rooms, executive suites, and a manicured landscape for its guests.

Above:
The conversion of Monmouth into a contemporary inn involved the installation of such amenities as a comfortable cocktail bar in the rear of the house.

Below:
A moody, late nineteenth-century photograph of Monmouth. Collection of Thomas H. Gandy and Joan W. Gandy.

Dunleith

CONSTRUCTED 1856

*S*cale is an essential element of high-style Natchez architecture, and Dunleith is a case in point. Its "peripteral" design – meaning that a row of columns surrounds the square building on all sides – makes it imposing enough, even before one counts the columns. And there are twenty-six of those, all of them colossal (they rise the height of two full stories). Everything else about Dunleith seems outsized, too, from its tall ceilings (15 feet) to its immense footprint (the building encloses some 9,500 square feet). And it sits amid a grand forty-acre landscape dotted with outbuildings, including two with the look of crenelated castles.

      Dunleith was built for a Pennsylvanian named Charles G. Dahlgren, who arrived from Philadelphia to work in the Natchez branch of

Even seen in the midst of its forty-acre landscape, Dunleith dominates its setting.

the Bank of the United States. At twenty-four, he was poised to make his fortune, and soon he married a well-to-do widow and became a planter. In 1835 he took up residence at Routhland, a fine Federal style home that had long been the home of his wife's family, the Rouths.

Dunleith was built on the site of that earlier house after lightning struck the original dwelling and it burned in 1855. Dahlgren and his wife commissioned Maryland-born designer John Crothers to build them the grand and up-to-date house that became Dunleith (originally Dahlgren's new home bore the name Routhland, too, but it was renamed during the Civil War era by a subsequent owner).

Dahlgren got to live in the house for only two years. His wife died and, honoring a promise he made her at the time of their marriage, he sold the property and distributed the proceeds to her children. Dahlgren would soon hold the rank of brigadier general in the Confederate Army of Mississippi, while a brother, John Dahlgren, became a rear admiral in the Union Navy.

Dunleith survived as a grand architectural display, with its two stories of broad and expansive porches. Even in its present incarnation as a bed-and-breakfast accommodation, there's a sense of bravado about the place, just as there is for some of the other grand Natchez mansions that were built at a time of growing internal conflict within the United States.

The furnishings at Dunleith are not original to the house, but the house is certainly well appointed. The dining room is decorated with pictorial Zuber wallpaper and a suitable range of period glassware and china.

The Grecian Mode

Above:
Today Dunleith's twelve rooms include eight guest rooms and generous modern appointments.

Left:
The double parlors at Dunleith are furnished with pierce-carved, Roccoco Revival furniture, a grand piano, and luxuriant window treatments, as well as marble, Renaissance Revival mantels and gilt overmantel mirrors.

The unforgettable Longwood, Natchez's tragic beauty.

CHAPTER 4

A More Modern Miscellany

ELMS COURT
SMITH-BONTURA-EVANS
STANTON HALL
MAGNOLIA HALL
EDGEWOOD
LONGWOOD

"Within three miles of the town the country is entirely occupied by houses and grounds of a villa character."
Frederick Law Olmsted, *A Journey in the Back Country*, 1860

The "Yeoman" visited Natchez in 1854. This anonymous correspondent was touring the South on behalf of the *New-York Daily Times* (a precursor of today's *New York Times*). His assignment was to send home regular reports describing everyday life in the region.

He was a Connecticut Yankee with the air of a gentleman. His manner was worldly, as he had only recently returned from a trip abroad that he chronicled in a book, *Walks and Talks of an American Farmer in England* (1852). His heavy mustache belied his relative youth (he was thirty-one), but his broad shoulders and robust good health suggested he was capable of a good day's work back home on his farm on Staten Island, New York, where he had established a nursery of fruit trees.

Though his readers didn't know it, the "Yeoman" was actually Frederick Law Olmsted, the man we regard today as the first and greatest American landscape architect, the creator of New York's Central Park, Boston's Emerald Necklace, the Stanford University Campus, and innumerable other revered landscapes. But in 1854 he was recovering from a failure in love – the woman who had promised him her hand had suddenly withdrawn it with little explanation – and he was still working to shape a larger vision of his work and his own future.

One qualification that had led the *Daily Times* editor to dispatch Olmsted was the fact he was not an abolitionist. Slavery was far and away the most contentious issue of the day, and Olmsted's brief was to report objectively on what he saw. He held a middle position with regard to slavery, thinking it unnatural and even unconstitutional; but, equally, he believed that its immediate abolition would both destroy his country and create a vast pool of illiterate, dependent Negroes who were ill prepared for citizenship. He went on his journey to earn his fees (ten dollars per article) and to see the South firsthand.

He arrived in Natchez on his stallion Belshazzar, having traveled north after visits to Baton Rouge and New Orleans. As he approached Natchez, he noted the richness of the soil and the beauty of the countryside. "The land," he wrote, "[is] almost all inclosed in plantations, the roadside boundaries of which are old rose-hedges."

In his travels, he rarely revealed he was a journalist and, being a natural mimic, at times adopted a convincing Southern accent. He reported having the following exchange before reaching Natchez:

"What sort of country is it, then, between here and Natchez?"

"Big plantations, sir, nothin' else," he was told.

"Do the planters . . . live on their plantations?" he inquired.

"Why a good many of them has two or three plantations," was the reply, "but they don't often live on any of them. Must have ice for their wine, you see, or they'd die; and so they have to live in Natchez or New Orleans."

Olmsted described the planters' rural residences as "cottages or very simple and unostentatious mansions." As he reached the town, however, he noticed that their character changed. "Within three miles of the town the country is entirely occupied by houses and grounds of a villa character," he wrote. He admired the trees and low bushes ("the best hedges and screens of evergreen shrubs that I have seen in America") but little else about the suburban residences impressed him. "The grounds usually exhibit . . . a paltry taste, with miniature terraces, and . . . no regard to architecture and landscape considerations. . . . The houses are not remarkable." As he approached his hotel, he was further disappointed. "The houses and shops within the town itself are generally small, and always inelegant," he concluded.

Given the genius he later revealed for shaping large landscapes, perhaps it's only appropriate that it was a natural vista that he liked best. "The grand feature of Natchez is the bluff," he reported, "terminating in an abrupt precipice over the river, with the public garden upon it. . . . I entered a gate and walked up a slope, supposing that I was approaching the ridge or summit of a hill . . . [but] I found myself . . . on the very edge of a stupendous cliff, and before me an indescribably vast expanse of forest. . . .

"Through the otherwise unbroken forest," he continued, "the Mississippi had opened a passage for itself, forming a perfect arc. . . . Overlooked from such an eminence, the size of the Mississippi can be realized. . . . [It] at once shamed all my previous conceptions of the appearance of the greatest of rivers."

Olmsted saw Natchez as an outsider. He was thrilled by the beauty of its setting and disappointed by its homes and gardens. He was a bit bemused by rich and idle young men he met, "dressed like New York clerks on their Sunday excursions, all lounging or sauntering, and often calling at the bar; all smoking, all twisting little walking-sticks, all 'talking horse.' " But he was quickly able to see what Natchez denizens could not – or would not – acknowledge. He reported back

The sunken terrace today behind Edgewood, Natchez's purest Italianate villa.

to his readers of the lack of diversity in its agriculture, its exclusive focus on cotton, recognizing it as a tragic flaw that would have a terrible future impact.

Any future fall seemed impossibly far away in 1850s Natchez. Cotton prices had risen and fallen over the years, but in the decade before the Civil War the price peaked. Production was up, too, and the Natchez district accounted for about 10 percent of the cotton produced in the entire South. It was a time for opulence and display in this remote outpost on its bluff overlooking the Mississippi.

The Grecian remained the architectural style of choice, but in the late 1850s other influences were felt, too. The Italianate in particular was the rage elsewhere, and it made some inroads in Natchez. One high-style example, Edgewood (see page 181), was built a few miles north of Natchez on a large, well-established plantation, but the Italianate influence was also apparent at one of Natchez's finest Greek Revival mansions. While Stanton Hall has the geometry of the Grecian style, its tall and imposing portico is accompanied by the brackets and lacy ironwork characteristic of the more ornamented Italianate (page 167).

When the Civil War began, construction came to a halt in Natchez, and attempts to be stylish seemed suddenly irrelevant. One house in particular was caught in the architectural equivalent of the playground game of statue; it's a freeze frame that today looks very much as it did in 1861 when its Yankee construction crew abruptly left. The immense Longwood (see page 185) is a monument to ruin, and of what came after the war, but still a rich demonstration of the astonishing affluence of the pre-Civil War years.

Elms Court

CONSTRUCTED CIRCA 1836
REMODELED CIRCA 1852

Built about 1836, the original house at Elms Court probably resembled a good many other mansions of its time. A two-story wooden structure, it had Grecian porticoes at the front and back and a wide center passage in between. But that was before it became a wedding present.

After the house was given to Jane Surget and Ayres P. Merrill in 1852 by her father, the newlyweds hired Thomas Rose to expand the home. Rose, who would later build Stanton Hall and Edgewood, literally left his signature ("T. Rose") on a beam at Elms Court. He devised a plan

A 1960s renovation transformed what was built as the billiard room into this comfortable library. The portrait over the mantel is of David McKittrick, the owner who opened the house to the public for the first Natchez Pilgrimage in 1932.

incorporating new single-story, stucco-on-masonry wings on either side of the existing block and a twelve-foot addition to the rear. The remodeled house would be finished with a mix of the original Grecian wood trim and Italianate and other decorative details. The remodeled Elms Court would have twenty-two rooms, including a billiard hall, smoking room, music room, and double parlors, amounting to more than five thousand square feet of living space.

The exterior transformation was dramatic, too. The front portico was replaced by a deep, two-tiered gallery that covered the face of the original house. It was flanked by matching one-story galleries that lined the new wings. The result was a 142-foot-long porch that provides protection from sun and rain like those at so many Natchez homes. But the scale and the material used makes Elms Court's galleries unique. The linked galleries across the entire façade also unify the long and rather awkward set of three structural blocks.

The house sits amid a landscaped site of about 150 lush acres at the edge of Natchez. It has remained in the same family since 1852, though it was given a second time as a wedding present, once again to a Surget daughter, in 1895.

Above:
The ironwork porch defines the look of
Elms Court, softening and shading the
immensely long structure.

Left:
A bedroom at Elms Court with
twin beds, four-poster style.

A More Modern Miscellany

Despite their weight, the cast-iron railings and arches have a surprisingly delicate look, as their piercing allows for the interplay of light and shadow.

Smith-Bontura-Evans

CONSTRUCTED 1851

BALCONIES ADDED CIRCA 1890

Robert Smith was a free man of color. Born in Maryland, he came to Natchez in the 1830s and found work as a hackman. He maintained his status as a man of "unshackled condition" (in antebellum Mississippi, free blacks were required by law to demonstrate their good character to the Board of Police at three-year intervals), and by 1849 owned his own livery business. In 1851, he purchased a lot on which to build a house consistent with his professional success.

The home that Robert Smith built for himself says a good deal about the man. Certainly Smith wanted a solid and comfortable house, but he

Originally a one-story wood-frame porch lined the front façade of the house, but a subsequent owner added the two-story ironwork galleries, probably in the mid-1890s.

didn't set out to make a flashy design statement. The design was conservative, with short front halls and three rooms running front-to-back on each floor. Smith operated his taxi business out of a two-story, freestanding carriage house to the rear of the residence.

The setting of the house appealed to Robert Smith because it was situated near the road connecting Natchez Under-the-Hill to the town on the bluff, meaning Smith could conveniently serve the needs both of the per-

Robert Smith maintained a workshop, as well as his horses, in the carriage house behind the house he built on Broadway.

manent inhabitants uptown and the transients who came and went from below. The next owner, Joseph Bontura, opened an inn. Again the convenience of the site to the riverside steamship docks was good for business, and many visitors found accommodations at this house on Broadway.

For a time in the twentieth century, the Smith-Bontura-Evans home was the property of the National Society of Colonial Dames, but it once again is privately owned. The Smith-Bontura-Evans house is a Pilgrimage fixture, a rare example of both a mixed-use residential-commercial complex and a middle-class, free black man's prosperity in antebellum Mississippi.

Above left:
The panoramic view of the
Mississippi from the porch of the
Smith-Bontura-Evans House.

Below left:
Among the famous people believed
to have found room and board at
Mr. Bontura's inn were Samuel
Clemens and Stephen Foster.

Stanton Hall

CONSTRUCTED 1851-1857

After Stanton Hall was completed in 1857, contemporary accounts called it "palatial" and "princely." In a town where the overwrought had become the rule, Stanton Hall gave the word mansion new meaning. The largest house in Natchez, it dominates the cityscape from the top of its own hill. Today it survives – along with the ghostly Longwood – as a reminder of the city's last and most ostentatious display of prosperity.

Everything about Stanton Hall is overstated. The doors are ten feet tall. The two main floors account for almost 11,000 square feet of living

Though built in downtown Natchez, Stanton Hall does not seem cramped in the midst of its expansive site, a full city block.

Left: Stanton Hall was built of brick that was stuccoed and painted white, then richly decorated with a variety of sculptural details. Note the date (1857) and the decoration in the pediment.

Right: Though screened by the capitals on the upper level of the portico, the grounds are dominated by live oaks. It is said that the man for whom the house was built, Frederick Stanton, planted nineteen of them when the property was cleared for construction in the 1850s. Seventeen survive today.

space, excluding the other three levels, which include the basement, third-floor storage rooms, plus a belvedere on the roof containing a billiard room with a sweeping view of the city and the Mississippi River.

The house was built and probably designed by Thomas Rose. His plans were hardly revolutionary, even for Natchez. Its geometry is a variation on the theme of Rosalie, as Stanton Hall shares the basic configuration of that earlier house, including the bold columned portico; broad open halls down the center that extend the full depth of the house; and the dual galleries across the back. Yet Stanton Hall is far from a copy of Rosalie.

On the east side of Stanton Hall the two-story porch is defined by lacy cast-iron rails and arches.

The proportions are Grecian, with the usual bulky, post-and-lintel character to its lines and masses. But some elements have been elaborated, such as the cast-iron Corinthian columns on the portico, and many updated details were applied to the rectangular forms, some of them adopted from a popular builder's book of the time, *The Beauties of Modern Architecture* by New Yorker Minard Lafever. Tastes were changing, and Renaissance Revival arches with carved foliage punctuate the hall and decorate Carrara marble mantels. Lacy forms adorn the ironwork on the porches. Victorian tastes were emerging, softening the severity of the Greek Revival. Surface details had been banished at the

One of the set of three grand parlors that line the east side of Stanton Hall. As befits the space, the carpet is English Axminster, the window treatments are executed with Schumacher fabric from the Historic Natchez Collection, and the original marble-topped window seat came from the Belter workshops of New York.

height of the Greek Revival – their absence is apparent in the hard lines of a house like Melrose – but they returned in the 1850s.

Stanton Hall was built for Frederick Stanton, a planter and cotton broker. He had emigrated from Ireland in 1815, and he named his house Belfast (the place would be renamed Stanton Hall much later). Residing nearby at Cherokee, he watched his palatial mansion rise. When he moved in, he staffed the mansion with seventeen house slaves but despite his great wealth – his holdings included 444 slaves and 15,109 acres of land spread over six plantations – he got to live in his dream house for only a short time before his death in January of 1859. His widow lasted a good deal longer, spending the next thirty-four years there. Built on an almost institutional scale, the house was well adapted for its next incarnation as the Stanton College for Young Ladies, during which time the name Stanton Hall came into use. It once again become a private home in 1904.

Having been one of the early stops on the Pilgrimage as a residence, Stanton Hall was purchased in 1938 by the Pilgrimage Garden Club. The Garden Club members aimed to turn it

The central hall is seventy-two feet long and sixteen feet wide with seventeen-foot ceilings.

into their headquarters, as well as a permanent house museum, much as their competitors at the Natchez Garden Club had done with the nearby House on Ellicott's Hill. Stanton Hall needed restoration; it was empty of furnishings; it required both study and interpretation. To raise money, Stanton Hall became the site for dances and overnight guests were accommodated during the early years of the Garden Club's ownership.

In Natchez, the present has a way of referencing the past, and Stanton Hall has its moments *déjà vu*. The stalwart lady who led the efforts at Stanton Hall — as she had done in helping found the Pilgrimage a half-dozen years earlier — was Katherine Grafton Miller. She happened also to be a great-granddaughter of Captain Thomas Rose, the home's builder-designer.

In keeping with the gargantuan scale of the house, the dining room is thirty-five feet long.

Right:
Immediately inside the front door was an office for the man of the house. The elaborately carved Rococo Revival
desk belonged to Frederick Stanton, having been recently returned to the house by one of his descendants.

Below:
One of the six bedrooms on the second floor at Stanton Hall. While some of the furniture in the house
belonged to the Stantons, most was acquired from other sources, since the original objects were dispersed at
the turn of the twentieth century

A More Modern Miscellany

Magnolia Hall

CONSTRUCTED 1858-1859

As the last mansion built in downtown Natchez before the Civil War, Magnolia Hall sums up the architectural trends of the time. Like Stanton Hall, it is a Grecian variation on the Rosalie plan; again like Stanton Hall, Magnolia has enough Victorian variations that its rigid classical lines seem softer. In particular, the reddish hue of the walling at Magnolia Hall, meant to resemble brownstone, gives this imposing house a surprising warmth.

The man for whom it was built, Thomas Henderson, also conforms to a common Natchez profile. He made his money in cotton, both as a cot-

Magnolia Hall was constructed of brick which was then covered with stucco, and painted and scored to look like brownstone. The columns supporting the immense portico are Ionic, but Italianate touches abound, including the brackets, front-entry arches, and cast-iron rails.

ton factor and as a planter. Though his merchant business was in New Orleans and Natchez and his plantations were across the river in Concordia Parish, Henderson built this house in Natchez for his considerable family. An existing house on the site, which had belonged to Henderson's father, a Scots immigrant, was moved a short distance down the street.

With some ten thousand square feet of living space, Henderson's house could comfortably accommodate the widower Henderson and several other adult Hendersons, including a maiden sister who was charged with the upbringing of his children. The plan at Magnolia Hall incorporates twelve rooms in the main house (three rooms on either side of the main halls, upstairs and down), as well as a ten-room service wing attached to the rear of the house. Contrary to the style of most other antebellum mansions in Natchez, the main staircase is located in the central hall.

Originally known as the Henderson House, it became the Britton House during the ownership of a prominent Natchez banker named Britton. It remained a residence until 1935, when it became the Magnolia Inn, which rented rooms to a well-heeled clientele. Later it spent a decade as the Trinity Episcopal Day School, but in 1976 it was donated to the Natchez Garden Club. Magnolia Hall has since been opened to the public as a house museum, with furnishings and finish based upon the inventory prepared at Henderson's death in 1866.

The dining room at Magnolia Hall (foreground) was entered from the central passage through the pocket doors. The kitchen was in an attached wing.

Edgewood

CONSTRUCTED 1859-1860

A private road meanders toward the center of Edgewood's ninety-acre tract. Lined with old cedars and moss-laden oaks, the route follows the rise and fall of the topography. Then the house itself appears, a large, graceful splash of soft color. Unlike many fine suburban villas in Natchez, Edgewood's plantation setting, seven miles north of the city, is countrified and quiet.

The first owner of the house, Samuel H. Lambdin, was a Pennsylvanian who became a steamboat commander on the Mississippi. Later a banker and planter, he married Jane Bisland, a member of a long-established Natchez family. The home they commissioned was built on the southeast edge

The exterior of the house is stucco on brick, painted to look like stone. Its color is known locally as "Edgewood peach."

of the large Bisland plantation. They hired the New Orleans architectural firm of Howard & Diettel to design the house; to build it, they contracted with Thomas Rose, the veteran builder of Stanton Hall.

As constructed in 1859-60, the house had all the modern conveniences, including indoor plumbing and speaking tubes. The style of the place — many of its details are Italianate — also suggests the owners' desire to be current. The Italianate had become widely popular elsewhere in the United States in the 1850s, and the deep eaves supported by brackets and the arch-topped window at center front on the second story are

characteristic elements. But the design of Edgewood is hardly a radical departure from other Natchezian homes of the time. The towers so characteristic of the Italianate style elsewhere weren't adopted by the designers of Edgewood. Instead the house has a more traditional five-bay shape and a front entrance that is Grecian with pilasters and sidelights. It's a thoughtful blend of the new and the traditional.

Set atop its small rise, Edgewood appears to be two stores tall, but its basement opens at grade level to the rear. Inside there are many familiar Natchez elements: The rooms are grand in scale, the mantels of marble, and the ceilings feature elaborate plaster cornices and medallions. Two attached service wings extend from the rear.

Edgewood was in the hands of Lambdin descendants until well into the twentieth century. Today, amid its peaceful setting of lush plantings and framed by ancient oaks, it remains a private home.

Above left:
The front porch at Edgewood is lined with wooden columns topped by cast-iron Corinthian capitals. It surveys the grounds which remain open and generous.

Far Left:
The comfortable den at Edgewood, with an eclectic array of objects reflecting the owners' travels.

Left:
The floor plan at Edgewood differs slightly from what had become the Natchez norm as the stairway, rather than being tucked into a side hall, dominates the central passage.

Longwood

As the decade turned, so did the fortunes of Natchez. The high prices fetched by cotton in the 1850s seems to have induced a blindered euphoria; even a man with the business acumen of Haller Nutt — a "scientific farmer" and progressive planter — failed to heed the warnings. War seemed more inevitable by the day, and the United States's cotton monopoly was breaking down, with imports arriving from Egypt, China, and India. Yet on Christmas Eve, 1859, Nutt wrote to his Philadelphia architect announcing his intention to begin construction of Longwood. Not so many years later, that house would come to be known as "Nutt's Folly."

Longwood may resemble a finished house — but a look inside reveals a vacant shell.

Bare brick, exposed timbers, and temporary scaffolding are all signs of construction left unfinished — or, in this case, abandoned.

Upon receiving Nutt's letter, architect Samuel Sloan immediately traveled to Natchez. In the meantime, Nutt had assigned more than twenty slaves to prepare timber, begin the foundation excavation, and fire the first bricks. The plans were completed by April and in May masons, too, arrived from Philadelphia. Within weeks window frames, brackets, tin roofing material, and columns for the house were being offloaded at the docks. More decorative trim was soon being produced in Natchez itself by seventy skilled millworkers Sloan had sent. In less than a year, however, Mississippi had seceded and the workman from the North were making their way home across the battle lines.

The house they left behind looked impressive from the exterior, since Longwood's masonry envelope and tin roof were virtually complete. But the interior remained empty, a brick

Looking directly upward into Longwood's lantern, six stories above.

shell perforated by the gaping window frames. There were no finished floors and no plaster partitions, just the vast bare skeleton of the pine frame.

While the house remained far from complete in 1861, Sloan published finished renderings of Longwood that year as "Design I– Oriental Villa" in his architectural plan book *Homestead Architecture*. Intended to evoke visions of Persian palaces and *The Arabian Nights*, the design was of an amalgam of Italianate and Moorish elements. But Longwood doesn't truly resemble anything but itself. Its enormous eight-sided footprint is 104 feet across, enclosing some 30,000 square feet of living space (the average new home in the United States today contains fewer than 2,000 square feet). Its perimeter was punctuated by 8 verandas and 4 porches. The plans called for 115 doors, 26 fireplaces, 24 closets, and windows 11 feet tall. The design was tailored to the family's needs, with

There are paint pots and an abandoned workbench inside Longwood. They've been there since before the war — the Civil War, that is, almost a century and a half ago.

bedrooms for the eight Nutt children, grand parlors, a central rotunda open to the cupola six stories above, and a library for Haller Nutt's collection of 10,000 volumes. It was a house fit for a planter king like Haller Nutt who, by 1860, had assembled a small empire of plantations in Louisiana and Mississippi that represented total holdings of some 800 slaves and 40,000 acres of land.

The result was to have been a summer home with thirty-two rooms and a household that included thirty-two servants, but the Civil War altered even Nutt's circumstances. By 1862 the Nutt family was in residence at Longwood, though they lived only in the nine-room basement. The revised plan called for completion of the house after the war, but by the time hostilities ended, Haller Nutt was dead. As his wife reported:

On June 16th, 1864, I buried my husband. He had gone to Vicksburg . . . and taking pneumonia died suddenly. But it was not Pneumonia that killed him. The doctor said it was not. It was his troubles. Three million dollars worth of property swept away; the labor of a life time gone; large debts incurred by the War pressing on him, and his helpless wife with eight children and two other families looking to him for support. All were reared in the lap of luxury and now utter poverty stood before them. This crushed him and he died.

In 1897 Julia Nutt, too, would die in one of those basement rooms.

The uncompleted house was owned by Nutt descendants until 1968. Virtually unchanged, it remains

The cellar was hurriedly finished for the Nutts during the early months of the Civil War. These temporary quarters, however, proved to be permanent.

today on its 86 acres two miles south of Natchez, an uninhabited masonry shell. It's a museum house owned and administered by the Pilgrimage Garden Club; and it is a metaphor for the precipitous fall of Natchez.

The house is over the top, to say the least. Its outlandish shape, its eclectic details, and its gigantic proportions suggest that fancy gave way to foolishness, particularly given the times and the economic climate. As an architectural site, Longwood is in select company. Few buildings have the impact that Longwood does upon its visitors — perhaps that theatricality may explain why it is Natchez's most visited house by far. Its preternatural quiet isn't like that of any other construction site; it's impossible at Longwood to imagine that the workers will be back from lunch any time soon — or ever.

The basement dining room seems grand enough (the dimensions are eighteen feet by twenty-four) but not compared to what was planned. The architect's renderings laid out a thirty-two room house, including a "sun parlor" on the fifth-level balcony and an observatory on the sixth.

Longwood is certainly a folly. Along with the Sun King's Versailles and Ludwig of Bavaria's Neuschwanstein, Longwood is also an architectural metaphor for cultural excess. An age was ending but Haller Nutt found himself carried by an economic tide he was unable to escape before the wave crashed upon the rocks.

Monteigne, an Italianate cottage built before the Civil War, as remodeled in the 1920s.

CHAPTER 5

After the Fall

GLEN AUBURN
GLENBURNIE
MONTEIGNE
EDELWEISS
MYRTLE BANK

"The great houses of Natchez, Mississippi . . . are enormous in scale, ceiling height, and room size; lavish in interior trim, at times to the point of lush decadence; palatial rather than domestic, and accurately disclosing a kind of economic unbalance that could not last."
Talbot Hamlin, *Greek Revival Architecture in America*, 1944

Although most Natchez voters opposed secession, the state of Mississippi followed the lead of South Carolina and on January 9, 1861, it became the second state to secede. The following month Jefferson Davis, a Mississippian, became president of the Confederate States of America. A Union blockade was soon established and, with little cotton being exported, the dominant source of income produced few dollars. The Emancipation Proclamation freed the slaves officially on January 1, 1863, but that was only one factor in the decline of Natchez fortunes.

Unlike Vicksburg or Richmond, Natchez never became the scene of a great siege. When Vicksburg fell so did Natchez, as there was no army to defend it (by then Natchez was inhabited by women, children, and men too old or infirm for military service). The splendid homes had no military significance, though the Union Army did demolish one fine house atop the bluff just north of town in order to establish Fort McPherson and take strategic advantage of an elevated view of the river. But occupying Union troops did relatively little harm, and at the close of the war, some of their number departed with the affection and respect of the townspeople.

The outcome of the war may have been predetermined — one reason some of Natchez's wealthiest men opposed secession was their recognition that an agrarian society was ill-equipped to defeat an industrial nation. But after the war, Natchez's predominant economic engine remained stalled. Cotton would never recover its momentum, as there were disastrous

A comfortable Victorian streetscape in Natchez's Clifton Heights neighborhood.

crop failures in 1866 and 1867, and new competition from imported Egyptian cotton. The slaves had been freed, but since there was no redistribution of land, those who remained became sharecroppers. In a time of falling prices, neither planters nor individual growers were getting rich off the produce of the land.

The nature of the prewar prosperity deepened postwar hardships. Just as the one-crop agriculture had depleted the soil, the devotion to cotton had stunted other economic development. Few planters had invested in manufacturing or infrastructure; the absence of other goods to sell and of railroad service were major factors in the decline in Natchez fortunes. The Natchez Trace, the nationally known trail linking the city to Nashville 450 miles away, remained unimproved and had fallen into disuse by 1820. By the middle 1830s, a rail line had linked New Orleans, Nashville, and Chicago — but its route had been via Jackson, bypassing Natchez. Though still served by regular steamboat service, post-Civil War Natchez had become isolated, unlike the nearby rail towns of Vicksburg and Port Gibson. The efficiencies of rail transport would soon render the riverboat obsolete for the shipment of goods.

Before the Civil War, most planters had invested the bulk of their financial gains in land and chattel. Planters like Stephen Duncan were the exception: Certainly, he got rich growing cotton but, unlike most planters, he diversified. When he left Natchez for good in 1863 to return home to New York, his enormous fortune included major holdings in northern securities, in particular railroad bonds. For the planters who relied solely upon cotton, the best of times were followed by the worst of times.

The city of Natchez had been poised to become a powerhouse, not only economically but politically, as well, when it had become the capital of the newest state in the Union in 1817. But the business of politics, too, had been allowed gradually to drift away after the government moved to Jackson in 1822. The illusion that Natchez was the cultural and economic capital of the state remained but after the war the pretense was quickly revealed. The stunted growth of the place was reflected in its population: In an era of enormous growth for the nation and, in particular, the Mississippi valley, Natchez's population went from 1,400 at the turn of the nineteenth century to barely triple that fifty years later.

Yet life didn't end in Natchez with the Civil War. There were people who prospered in the years after, many of them merchants. While the planters built no new mansions, a few of the bankers and entrepreneurs were able to afford new, in-town homes. Many of the arrivals were from the north, not a few of them Jewish (Mississippi's first synagogue, Temple B'Nai Israel, was constructed in Natchez in 1870-72). These men brought with them credit, long essential to the cotton economy, but in short supply in the South after the Civil War. By the end of the nineteenth century, Natchez had three banks, two cotton mills, two cottonseed mills, two lumber mills, a brick kiln, and a foundry. The commercial buildings in the Natchez business district reflect late nineteenth-century tastes. The town had finally managed to diversify, but there were no sources of wealth of the magnitude of prewar cotton. Then, once and for all, King Cotton was slain by the arrival of an agricultural pest, the boll weevil, in 1907.

Most of the antebellum houses of Natchez survived; and a few new ones joined them in the later nineteenth century. The abandoned site of Fort McPherson just north of town had been subdivided and a comfortable new residential neighborhood developed. Clifton Heights filled with commodious Victorian homes with river views for the merchant class that came to town. Other modest, modern dwellings in a variety of Victorian styles filled in gaps in the streetscape, among them Edelweiss (see page 213). Constructed in 1875, the grand Glen Auburn was perhaps the only new home of a size and grandeur to compete with the planters' mansions (see page 197). Some existing pre-Civil War homes were updated, too, including Myrtle Bank in the 1880s, Glenburnie at the turn of the twentieth century, and Monteigne in the 1920s (see pages 214, 201, and 205, respectively). If its best days were behind it, Natchez still found a way to maintain some semblance of its pride.

Glen Auburn

CONSTRUCTED 1875

After a lapse of almost twenty years, a major new house was constructed in Natchez in 1875. The rules had changed, thanks to the Civil War and falling cotton prices, producing a seismic shift in the local economy. One result was that the new mansion in town would not be the home of a planter but of a newly arrived businessman.

The owner of Glen Auburn was Christian Schwartz. He was one of a group of merchants and financiers who reshaped business in Natchez. The means to wealth would no longer be cotton – it became credit – and Schwartz and the other new arrivals guided the businesses downtown to a

The Second Empire style was well adapted to downtown houses like this one, Glen Auburn, on Natchez's Commerce Street.

The parlor at Glen Auburn, with its mix of high Victorian (note the wallpaper border) and antebellum elements (the gilt mirror over the mantel).

new level of prosperity. The plantations in the countryside, now worked by sharecroppers rather than slaves, no longer produced pots of money.

Schwartz's house, named Glen Auburn, was constructed in the French Second Empire style. The mansard roof is the defining characteristic: The roofline slopes at an almost flat pitch only to become nearly vertical upon approaching the eaves (the flatter pitch of the roof is usually not visible from ground level). The roof, named after Renaissance architect

Glen Auburn's central hall. The through passage, extending front-to-back, remained a fixture in Natchez planning even after the Civil War.

François Mansard, was adopted for the wings added to the Louvre in Paris after 1852; the style became associated with the Second Empire, as the reign of Napoleon III (1852-1871) was known.

Glen Auburn is a textbook example, with a square tower at the center of its façade; two principal floors with a tall attic story fronted by dormers; bold brackets around its eaves; double entrance doors; tall narrow windows with arched tops; and ornate ironwork cresting that defines the upper roofline. It's a grand wedding cake of a house, a fitting testament to a new bold prosperous presence in Natchez.

Descendants of Christian Schwartz remained in residence until 1903. The house has changed hands numerous times since and, in the 1990s, was opened as a bed-and-breakfast, its interiors chockablock with Renaissance Revival and Eastlake style Victorian furniture. More recently, new owners have fitted out the place with older Empire and Grecian furniture that gives the house an old Natchez feel despite its postwar date. It is almost as if there's a gravitational pull exerted, drawing the houses of Natchez, whatever their dates of construction, back to the city's antebellum heyday.

Glenburnie

CONSTRUCTED 1833

REMODELED 1900

Glenburnie is one Natchez house that hasn't remained frozen in time. While it retains much antebellum character, a sympathetic addition during the Colonial Revival era significantly enlarged the home.

Glenburnie was one of the last Natchez houses built in the Federal style with a central passage, flanked by a pair of rooms, with a larger room to the rear. In its original incarnation the basic elements of the planter's cottage were still very much in evidence: The house was one story tall, with a deep gallery recessed beneath its roof, and a fine Federal entrance with sidelights and an elliptical fan sash above.

The 1833 house consisted of the right-hand portion of today's larger dwelling; the projecting portico on the left fronts the 1900 addition.

From the side, the circa 1900 addition to Glenburnie with its familiar Natchez gallery.

The renovators wisely decided to adopt the same architectural forms. Thus the two-room addition (producing a T-shaped plan) is surrounded by galleries supported by Tuscan columns echoing those of the original structure. The new kitchen and great room updated the house, but felt at one with the rest. Today the house has a bright, clean, and fresh quality. Decorated with antiques like those that would have been found there in the nineteenth century, there is an apparent respect for the past.

*The entry passage hall at
Glenburnie, with the promise
of the rear parlor beyond.*

Monteigne

CONSTRUCTED 1855

REMODELED 1927

*M*onteigne has lived a double life. At the time of its initial construction in 1855, it was a picturesque cottage, built in the spirit of what A.J. Downing, author of the influential *The Architecture of Country Houses* (1850), called the "Cottage-Villa." It was Italianate in style, nearly cubic in shape, its rooflines decorated with brackets, and its front lined with a porch. Then, three-quarters of a century later, the house was given a face lift.

The new impression was haughtier, with high-style neoclassical detailing. Although the basic block of the house remained little changed, the 1927 remodeling replaced the original gallery across the front with a tall,

The proud façade of Monteigne, as reinvented in 1927.

After the Fall

The lush plantings that surround Monteigne are set off by walls and other hardscape.

pedimented portico. An arched entranceway was added, as were semicircular inset panels over the windows on the front. The bracketed roofline was classicized with a molded cornice. The allusion to the grace and ease of the Tuscan countryside was superseded by the formality of Parisian neoclassicism.

The change outside was reflected in the interior. A grand and graceful stairway was added in the central hall; what once were double parlors to its left were opened into a single deep and impressive space. Certain details survive from the 1855 original, among them door frames and some of the mantels, but are overshadowed by the added elements, which include fine French scenic wallpaper in the hall.

The twenty-three acres surrounding the house have been elaborately landscaped. Literally hundreds of varieties of camellias and a range of other ornamental plants provide a colorful setting for a house quite unlike any other in Natchez.

Right:
The single parlor, as remodeled in 1927, which made it an expression of its time, an era when fewer families in Natchez had the means to make grand architectural statements.

Below:
This enfilade view across the front of Monteigne suggests that, despite its modest exterior, this is a spacious and grand house.

Left:
The staircase, the wallpaper, and the running-diamond floor all arrived with
the New Orleans architectural firm of Weiss, Dreyfus, and Seiferth in the
twentieth century.

Below:
The splendidly outfitted dining room at Monteigne, just off the rear hall.

Edelweiss

CONSTRUCTED 1883

The streets of Natchez have a sampling of houses that suggest the diversity of Victorian architecture, and Edelweiss is an intriguing example. A merchant named Joseph O'Brien found the design in a plan book, *Illustrated Homes* by E.C. Gardner. Published in Boston in 1875, the book had a plate of this house, aptly labeled "the Planter's House." A generous gallery around three sides of the house is well adapted to the Natchez climate, but the picturesque character of the house is what makes it memorable. The Victorian chamfered trusswork of its gable and exposed rafters are both handsome and notable for their rarity in this predominantly antebellum town.

Once a rooming house with its porches enclosed, Edelweiss was opened up by the current owners — it had been become thirteen separate and cramped compartments — who raised their family there. The name Edelweiss was given to the place in honor of a small, stylized relief carving of a flower in the newel post.

Far left:
The picturesque Edelweiss, lifted from the pages of a style book.

Left:
The view from the porch: The Edelweiss trusswork frames the view of the Mississippi.

Afterword

Natchez is a remarkable survivor. It's a unique place – to the uninitiated, it appears a very Southern town and certainly it is. Yet when you listen closely, the accents are softer. It is a place many young people leave for lack of economic opportunity; but a surprising number eventually return. Those that don't, it is said, really meant to.

Natchez is full of surprising juxtapositions. You can stand at the gas pumps at a Shell station and gaze upon Monmouth, a truly impressive antebellum mansion. Another such house, D'Evereux, fronts on a four-lane highway. A golf course and a children's playground crowd the backdoor of Auburn. The Briars is reached only via the parking lot of a Ramada Inn.

Natchez is also a place where people seem tied to their houses. I must admit to finding the reverence for the past strangely moving, especially at houses where the gardens are encroaching, the roofs are deteriorating, and there's decay on the porches (it's not accidental that Natchez is a city

At the top of a small rise stands Myrtle Bank, a modest dwelling constructed in the 1830s. Twenty years later it was adapted for use as a school for girls, but much of its curbside charm today is the result of a later adaptation. In the 1870s, new owners decided to give the galleried cottage a more contemporary character. The porch columns, railing, arched openings, and brackets were added, endowing the place with a distinctly Victorian character.

with multiple pest control contractors). It's become a job for some people – no, more than that, a life's work – to care for these places. It's their burden and their privilege.

The great mansions of Natchez are monuments to the concentration of wealth in the antebellum era, which produced a highly stratified society in which roughly one percent of the white citizens became planters with land and chattel. Yet today the wealth is more evenly distributed, and there are African-American citizens who are passionately involved in the preservation of Natchez.

The relationship between preservation and prosperity is often complex, although most well-preserved towns share a familiar story: A period of prosperity is followed by a radical downturn in fortune. Perhaps the railroad doesn't come through or the mines peter out. Whatever the specific cause, political, technological, and environmental factors conspire to change the rules. In the case of Natchez, the Civil War abruptly negated the generally accepted formula for success.

The people of Natchez found themselves with little ready cash. No doubt that was a rude shock, especially after the flush and carefree days before the Civil War. In retrospect, however, Natchez has hard times to thank for the survival of its wealth of architectural fabric. Without money to spend, the old styles survive; had the money continued to roll in Natchez would look very different, because its inhabitants would almost certainly have kept up with current

The Natchez City Cemetery was dedicated in 1822.

trends and attempted to outdo their neighbors. But in towns that find themselves largely forgotten and adrift in time, unspoiled buildings and streetscapes survive largely unchanged. Certainly that proved true in Natchez.

Even when the garden clubs came along in the 1930s, the limited funds available for restoration proved a long-term benefit to the city and its housing stock. The ladies of Natchez made an immense contribution in helping establish historic preservation as a laudable civic goal at a time when almost no one elsewhere recognized the wisdom in such thinking. A vague longing, in some cases a reverence for a more prosperous time, was turned to productive use. A social cachet came to be associated with the old houses; and, in practical terms, some of the profits from the Pilgrimage were distributed to homeowners for use in badly needed maintenance of their homes and gardens. But there still wasn't enough money to reinvent anything — which has proved to be important since even the professional help of that time, though it often came from prestigious architectural firms, tended to be of the we-know-better school.

Ironically, Natchez's tough times served its magnificent buildings well. While antebellum Natchez was an expression of building passion, its caretakers in the years since have brought to their responsibilities an intense pride of place, a commitment to remembering its past, and an adamant refusal to let the great days be forgotten. The result has been a rich medium for preservation. Looking backward is easier in a place like Natchez than elsewhere. The vestiges of the past are more obvious. Like a snake that swallowed its prey whole, Natchez's timeline has one prominent swelling, and that represents the antebellum years when Natchez was the jewel of the lower Mississippi valley.

Acknowledgments and Notes

A range of people, past and present, helped make this book possible. At the head of the list come the individuals who have invested themselves in caring for the fine homes of Natchez and who gave us permission to visit and photograph them. To begin, then, the homeowners.

They include, at Airlie, Katie and Terry Freiberger; Auburn, City of Natchez and Auburn Garden Club; Bontura, Ruth and James Coy III; The Burn, Ty and Sonja Taylor; The Briars, Newton Wilds and Robert E. Canon; Cherokee, Cynthia Bailey; Cottage Gardens, Jerold and Betty Jo Krouse; D'Evereux, Peggy and Jack Benson; Dunleith, René Adams; Edelweiss, Margaret Wesley; Edgewood, W. Bruce and Darleine Bucklew; Elms Court, Anne W.S. MacNeil and Elizabeth Boggess; Glen Auburn, Ann and Clifford Randolph Tillman; Glenburnie, Margaret and George Guido; Gloucester, John Deakle; Green Leaves, Virginia B. Morrison; Hawthorne, Bettye and Hyde Jenkins; Hope Farm, Ethel Green Banta; House on Ellicott's Hill, Natchez Garden Club; Lansdowne, Devereux Slatter and George Marshall IV; Linden, Jeanette Feltus; Longwood, Pilgrimage Garden Club; Melrose, National Park Service; Magnolia Hall, Natchez Garden Club; Monteigne, Mary Louise Shields; Monmouth, Ron and Lani Riches, owners, and Jean Luc Momis; Myrtle Bank, Thomas H. and Joan W. Gandy; Richmond, Lela Jeanne Nall; Rosalie, Mississippi Society of the Daughters of the American Revolution; Stanton Hall, Pilgrimage Garden Club; and Texada, Margaret Moss.

A number of other individuals were also essential to our attempt to understand Natchez, its history, and its houses. At the top of this list are Ronald W. Miller and Mary Warren Miller at the Historic Natchez Foundation; they are energetic, ever-patient, and always companionable sources of answers and ideas. John Saleeby as General Manager of Natchez Pilgrimage Tours gave generously of his time — and of his passion for his adopted home. In Jackson, Mississippi, Jennifer Baughn and Brenda Crooke at the Historic Preservation Division of the Mississippi Department of Archives and History provided entree to the Department's extensive files on Natchez. Our appreciation, too, to Joan W. and Dr. Thomas H. Gandy for permission to reproduce the period black-and-white images. In the publishing process, our thanks must go to Rizzoli publisher Charles Miers, who saw the wisdom in commissioning a book about Natchez; to editor Jane Ginsberg, who oversaw the production of the book; and to Jean Atcheson who brought her considerable editorial talents to bear in making the manuscript better.

In addition to the people, there were numerous books to which we made reference in learning many of the facts and stories recounted in this volume. One early visitor to Natchez who recorded his reactions was John James Audubon; for the account of his visit that appears in Chapter 2, the sources included *Audubon's America: The Narratives and Experiences of John James Audubon*, Donald Culross Peattie, editor (Boston: Houghton Mifflin Company, 1940); *The Life of John James Audubon, The Naturalist*, Mrs. John J. [Lucy] Audubon, editor (New York: G.P. Putnam's Sons, 1894); and Francis Hobart Herrick's *Audubon the Naturalist: A History of His Life and Time* (New York: D. Appleton-Century Company, 1938). In writing Chapter 3, an anonymous travelogue ("By a Yankee") titled *The South-West* (volume 2, New York: Harper & Brothers, 1835) was particularly useful. Its author was subsequently identified as Joseph Holt Ingraham; much of the book is devoted to his stay in Natchez and environs. The Frederick Law Olmsted vignette in Chapter 4 is based upon Olmsted's own *A Journey in the Back Country* (New York: G.P. Putnam's Sons, 1907, originally published in 1853-4 in the *New-York Daily Times* and collected first in book form in 1860); and Witold Rybczynski's *A Clearing in the Distance: Frederick Law Olmsted and America in the Nineteenth Century* (New York: Simon & Schuster, Inc., 1999).

There is a growing literature devoted specifically to Natchez. *Antebellum Natchez* by D. Clayton James (Baton Rouge: Louisiana University Press, 1968) is a sound and readable history of the place prior to the Civil War. Offering a somewhat less scholarly approach to the subject is *Natchez: An Illustrated History* by David G. Sansing, Sim C. Callon, and Carolyn Vance Smith (Natchez, Miss.: Plantation Publishing Company, 1992). The other books are primarily pictorial. Two small volumes by Nola Nance Oliver, *Natchez: Symbol of the Old South* and *This Too is Natchez* (New York: Hastings House, 1940 and 1953, respectively) were early illustrated books about Natchez. *Natchez* by J. Wesley Cooper, a large-format volume, followed (Southern Historical Publications, Inc., 1957). The most formidable of the illustrated volumes on Natchez remains *Great Houses of Natchez*, text Mary Warren Miller and Ronald W. Miller, photographs by David King Gleason (Jackson, Miss., and London: University Press of Mississippi, 1986), though *Classic Natchez: History, Homes, and Gardens* by Randolph Delehanty and Van Jones Martin (Savannah, Ga.: Martin-St. Martin, 1996) is another authoritative volume, drawing as the authors did on the Historic Natchez Foundation archive. Two guidebooks are also generally available, *The Grace and Grandeur of Natchez Homes* by Joseph Arrigo (Stillwater, Minn.: Voyageur Press, 1994) and the perennial *The Majesty of Natchez* by Steven Brooke (Gretna, La.: Pelican Publishing Company, Inc., 1969). Four collections of period photographs of Natchez have been published under the editorship of Joan W. and Thomas H. Gandy. They include: *Natchez: City Streets Revisited; Natchez: Landmarks, Lifestyles, and Leisure; Victorian Children in Natchez*; and *The Mississippi Steamboat Era in Historic Photographs* (Charleston, S.C.: Arcadia Publishing).

Other volumes address narrower aspects of Natchez history, including *The Black Experience in Natchez: 1720-1880* by Ronald L.F. Davis (Natchez, Miss.: Eastern National, 1994, 1999); *Charles Dahlgren of Natchez: The Civil War and Dynastic Decline* (Washington, D.C.: Brassey's, Inc., 2002); *The Emergence of the Cotton Kingdom in the Old Southwest* by John Hebron Moore (Baton Rouge: Louisiana University Press, 1988). The appendix of *The Trial of Levi Weeks* by Estelle Fox Kleiger (Chicago: Academy Chicago Publishers, 1989) contains the detailed letter Levi G. Weeks wrote to a Deerfield friend characterizing both Auburn and life in Natchez in 1812. Finally, *The Building of Longwood*, Ina May Ogletree McAdams, editor (Natchez, Miss.: Natchez Garden Club, 1972) tells the remarkable story of Longwood through surviving correspondence and construction documents.

Index of Names and Places

Page references in **boldface** indicate the page number of an illustration or its caption.

All sites are in Natchez, Mississippi, unless otherwise noted.